The Disability Discrimination Act:

INCLUSION

a workbook for building owners,
facilities managers and architects

John H. Penton

The Disability Discrimination Act:

INCLUSION

a workbook for building owners, facilities managers and architects

for Kristina

Acknowledgements

In preparing this publication I should like to express my appreciation of
the assistance and encouragement that I have received from the following:

The Centre for Accessible Environments, in particular Sarah Langton-Lockton
Compass Partnership, in particular Mike Hudson
The Council for the Care of Churches, in particular Jonathan Goodchild
St Albans Cathedral, in particular Andrew Anderson and Alfred Hagerman
The Department for Education and Employment, in particular Paul Lenssen
The Norfolk & Norwich NHS Health Care Trust, in particular Rob Smith
Healthgain (UK) Ltd, in particular Ken Morris
De Montfort University, Leicester, in particular Professor David Chiddick
and John Whitehead CBE

I would also like to thank Alaine Hamilton and Mark Lane at RIBA Publications,
and particularly David Rust for his meticulous and beautiful drawings.

© John Penton 1999

Published by RIBA Publications, Construction House, 56-64 Leonard Street, London, EC2A 4LT
ISBN 1 85946 032 1

Publisher: Mark Lane
Illustrations by David Rust, ©John Penton & David Rust 1999
Design by Terry Holland
Production by Kate Mackillop
Typesetting by The Design Agency
Printed and bound by Alden Press, Oxford

CONTENTS

LIST OF FIGURES

*   Also reproduced in 'Widening the Eye of the Needle: Access to Church Buildings for
     People with Disabilities' John Penton, published for the Council for the Care of Churches by
     Church House Publishing, 1999 (see Appendix A)

**   Also reproduced in 'Access for Disabled People to School Buildings: Management and
     Design Guide' Building Bulletin 91, published for the DfEE by The Stationery Office
     (Spring 1999, ISBN 0 11271 062 X; see Appendix A)

All design is a compromise, best reached by the study of man at his weakest.

A Aalto, 1942

1.00 INTRODUCTION: THE HISTORICAL CONTEXT OF THE ACT

1.01 In his 'Age of Extremes: the Short Twentieth Century' Eric Hobshawm describes the period between 1950 and 1980 as the 'Golden Age'. Even after the elapse of fifteen further years the Disability Discrimination Act 1995 is directly a product of that period.

1.02 The years following the Second World War saw fundamental changes in perceptions about disabled people and their place in society. The Beveridge Report of 1942 and the mass of legislation introduced by the Labour Governments of 1945 to 1951 were concerned with employment, health, housing and social and financial support for the individual. This reflected a fundamental shift in policies, away from segregation and separation, towards acceptance and recognition. However, even if these policy changes started to bring about change in attitudes about disability, there was little or no consultation with disabled people or their families. In consequence, these years saw the emergence of activist groups. It is easy to forget that The Spastics Society (now Scope), and already a national institution by the 1970s, was only formed in 1952 as a parent pressure group.

1.03 By the mid-1960s, post-war reconstruction was largely complete and the entire western world was enjoying an unparalleled surge in economic growth and prosperity - this was most spectacularly the case in the USA; but even in the UK incomes rose steadily, standards of living improved year on year, and expectations grew as a result. As part of that process people with disabilities began to challenge the stereotypical perceptions of them as different, special or incapable. Increasingly effective and articulate pressure groups exerted growing influence upon health and care professionals, and upon educators in both central and local government. Surveys were carried out and new definitions of disability were developed in order to be able to assess individual's needs and to respond to them with appropriate policies, services and benefits.

1.04 During the 1960s provision began to be made for 'special needs groups', for example in the form of special schools, and housing for elderly people. In 1963 Selwyn Goldsmith published the first edition of 'Designing for the Disabled' with the benefit of a grant from the Polio Foundation. For the first time basic design principles were set out to include access provision to buildings for wheelchair users and other disabled people. The British Standards Institute then published Code of Practice CP96, 1967: 'Access for the Disabled to Buildings'. This provided one of the essential tools which enabled Alf Morris to achieve the passage into legislation of his Private Members' Bill as the 'Chronically Sick and Disabled Persons Act, 1970' (CSDPA).

1.05 Those covered by the Act embraced a wide range of people. It applied to those 'who are substantially and permanently physically handicapped and also the mentally handicapped and mentally ill', and a duty was placed upon local authorities to identify the needs of people with these disabilities. Further duties were placed upon authorities to provide services and facilities which would improve the quality of life of disabled people, including welfare provision, housing and rehabilitation to enable people with disabilities to find employment. The requirements of the Act were couched in terms of what was 'practicable and reasonable' and it remained fundamentally flawed through the absence of any financial commitment to put its provisions in place. Nonetheless, its influence was profound and it became the platform on which subsequent legislation could be built.

1.06 During the 1970s people with disabilities became more assertive and such pressure groups as the Disablement Income Group contributed to making the general public more aware that disabled people form a normal component of society. In 1974 the DOE introduced the concept of Mobility Housing, followed by Wheelchair Housing in 1975. Funding was made available for both through the public sector building programmes with the declared objective of creating an increasingly large stock of housing that could be lived in, and which could also be visited, by people with disabilities. The Snowdon Report of 1977 recommended the integration of people with disabilities in the context of schools and hospitals and by local authorities. The Warnock Report of 1978 recommended that children with special needs should, whenever possible, receive their education in mainstream schools.

1.07 The International Year of Disabled People in 1980 was marked in the UK by the Disabled Persons Act 1981 which required that, when possible, 'appropriate provision' should be made for people with disabilities based on the new BS5810:1979, 'Access for the Disabled to Buildings', and DfE Building Note 18. Local authorities for the first time were required to bring the needs of people with disabilities, including those with sensory impairments, to the attention of Planning Applicants. In 1985, however, the Building Regulations were completely revised, and 1987 saw the introduction of 'Part M: Access and facilities for disabled people'. While this represented a fundamental change by establishing a regulatory basis for the provision of access its weakness was that it only applied to new buildings and to substantially separate extensions. Alterations to existing buildings and the management and operation of all buildings remained, as is still the case, outside the scope of Part M.

1.08 Nonetheless, a direct consequence of the introduction of Part M was the recognition that, if people with disabilities were increasingly to be present in buildings, provision would need to be made for their evacuation in the event of fire. This led to the publication of BS5588, Part 8:1988, 'Code of Practice for Means of Escape for Disabled People'. For the first time this Code of Practice, which subsequently was to become incorporated into Part B of the Building Regulations in 1992, recognised the fundamental conclusion that some people with disabilities will not be able to achieve evacuation from a building under their own power and therefore will need to be assisted.

1.09 Unlike Part M, Part B of the Building Regulations applies to all construction, whether new-build, or to extension, alteration and refurbishment. Again, uniquely, BS5588, Part 8 also includes the requirement for the establishment, operation and review of management evacuation strategies by building owners and managers.

1.10 In 1992, Part M was also completely revised, and greatly improved, largely as the result of a study by BSI, (PD5623:1989), which looked at comparable Regulations and Codes of Practice throughout the developed world. This led to the Part M Approved Document being restructured, stating the objectives of each section with clarity and providing supporting evidence for its subsequent recommendations. In this revised format the Approved Document represented a far more satisfactory body of guidance than had previously been the case; unfortunately it still only applied, in the main, to new-build situations.

1.11 Further restructuring has taken place with the issue of the 1999 Edition of Part M of the Building Regulations. The main changes in the 1999 Edition are:

- the extension of the application of Part M to new dwellings, including student living accommodation;

- defining the relationship between Part M and the Workplace (Health, Safety and Welfare) Regulations 1992, the Disability Discrimination Act 1995, and the Disability Discrimination (Employment) Regulations 1996;

- the addition of new sections 6 to 10 of the Approved Document setting out what are considered to be reasonable provisions in new dwellings; and

- the updating of references to standards, and other publications.

1.12 Attempts, originally initiated by the Dutch in the late 1980s, to develop a harmonised standard for Building Regulations in relation to 'Access and facilities for disabled people', applicable throughout the EU, have largely foundered, resulting only in the issue of the 'Final Draft' of the 'European Manual' in 1997. This document has suffered from too great a variation of views about acceptable standards, which currently differ widely across Europe, among the EU countries taking part in the development discussions. Perhaps more importantly there was also fundamental disagreement about which elements of the document should become mandatory in their application and which ones discretionary. As a result, the EU Commission does not regard the European Manual as forming an appropriate vehicle for the issue of a Directive.

1.13 During the 1970s and 1980s in the USA large numbers of the many disabled veterans who had survived the Vietnam War joined forces with activists of the Independent Living Movement to bring about radical change. This resulted in the 'Americans with Disabilities Act, 1992', (ADA). Effectively this was a change to the Constitution, establishing a new Civil Right of access to buildings in public use, and to publicly funded housing.

The Act has had, and continues to have, a profound effect, not only in the USA, but elsewhere in the developed world. In the UK this has proved to be particularly the case, and its influence has been extremely significant. Perhaps most interestingly it has also served to demonstrate the basic differences of approach between the establishment of civil rights of the individual and the laying down of ever more extensive regulations.

1.14 Meanwhile, the difficulties inherent in taking a regulatory approach to the alteration of existing buildings have remained seemingly insurmountable since the introduction of Part M in 1987, and in spite of the issue of the 1999 Edition. Indeed, it has increasingly become recognised that the Building Regulations do not provide an appropriate mechanism for determining the accessibility of existing construction or the management of premises in use. With the introduction of the Disability Discrimination Act, 1995 (DDA), an entirely new situation has been created in relation to the expectations, and now civil rights, of people with disabilities with regard to employment, the provision of services and access to the built environment.

1.15 Since 1995, with the introduction of the Act, the emergence of the concept of **inclusion** has rapidly gained momentum. Attitudes towards disabled people are changing fast, moving away from the perception of them as a distinct, homogeneous group for whom special provision should be made. Instead there is a turn towards the concept of an environment accessible to all, where disability is a normal component of the make-up of society. Such a concept necessarily embraces the entire built environment, both existing and yet to be constructed. This, in turn, means that the perception of acceptable, or 'reasonable' standards of provision will have to be reflected not just in how buildings and the spaces between them are designed, but also in how they are managed and operated.

1.16 The Disability Discrimination Act 1995, however imperfectly, has now created a 'civil right' of accessibility in the UK, vested in the individual. By the Act, and through the medium of common law and the establishment of precedent, disabled building users have been empowered to bring about change to the built environment and how it is managed.

2.00 THE DISABILITY DISCRIMINATION ACT 1995

2.01 The Disability Discrimination Act 1995 (DDA) outlaws discrimination against disabled people. It applies throughout the UK and is far reaching in embracing: employment; the provision of goods, facilities and services; and premises. It also relates to education and to public transport. The period for its implementation is unusual in extending over ten years from 1995 to the end of 2004.

2.02 In December 1997 the Government established a 'Disability Rights Task Force' (DRTF) and has now given a commitment, during 1999, to set up the 'Disability Rights Commission' (DRC). The remit of the DRC is seen as being:

To consider how best to secure comprehensive, enforceable civil rights for disabled people within the context of our wider society, and to make recommendations on the role and functions of a 'Disability Rights Commission' (DRC). To provide the latter by March 1998, and to provide a full report of its recommendations on wider issues no later than July 1999. The DRTF will take full account of the costs as well as the benefits of any proposals, as far as is quantifiable and practicable, and in particular ensure that its recommendations for a DRC achieve value for money for the taxpayer.

2.03 The DRTF has submitted its recommendations on the establishment of a Disability Rights Commission and a White Paper was published in July 1998. Once the DRC has been established the existing National Disability Council will cease to exist. The DRTF's final recommendations are to be submitted to the Government in July 1999 and are likely to propose the further expansion and strengthening of disability discrimination civil rights legislation.

2.04 The initial implementation of the Act and the establishment of the Disability Rights Commission now make it very clear that during the coming years the owners of premises, managers of facilities, and architects (as well as other building designers) will increasingly need to look at their buildings to ensure that they are made as fully accessible as possible. In that context the **Accessibility Appraisal** of the design in course of preparation, and the **Accessibility Audit** of the building in use are fundamental tools (see Section 3, and Appendix B).

2.05 As accessibility is an issue relating not only to how buildings are designed and built but also to how they are operated, managed and maintained, it may well be that the Guidance set out in Part M 1999 Edition, and the DfEE 1997 Constructional Standards are outweighed by the requirements of the DDA, whether or not construction is taking place. In the case of Listed Buildings, or those with the equivalent of Listing, such as churches and cathedrals, the publication of 'Easy Access to Historic Properties' by English Heritage has proved to be particularly helpful.

2.06 The definitions of disability under the provisions of the DDA are very broad. The Act defines disability as a physical and/ or mental impairment which has a substantial and long-term adverse effect on a person's ability to carry out normal day-to-day activities in one or more of the following areas:

- mobility;

- manual dexterity;

- physical co-ordination;

- continence;

- ability to lift, carry or otherwise move everyday objects;

- speech, hearing or eyesight;

- memory or ability to concentrate, learn or understand; and

- perception of the risk of physical danger.

2.07 The World Health Organisation (WHO), and the Office for Population Census & Surveys (OPCS), define a 'handicap' as the result of the interaction of a person's disability with their environment. As well as affecting those with the disabilities listed above, handicapping conditions of varying degrees of severity will also arise for:

- elderly people;

- those of excessively large or small stature;

- children;

- mothers-to-be in the later stages of pregnancy;

- parents and others in charge of small children, particularly those using pushchairs;

- those who are temporarily injured;

- those who are sick or ill;

- those who are emotionally distressed or unstable; and

- those who are laden with heavy luggage, particularly when held in both hands.

In view of the wide range of these conditions, it is of fundamental importance wholly to reassess the conventional, and indeed, often stereotypical pictures that we have of the population.

2.08 In setting out the above definitions of disability the Act covers not only people who have a disability, but people who have had a disability but no longer have one. In the guidance accompanying the Act examples of physical and mental impairments include:

- physical impairments affecting the senses such as sight and hearing; and

- mental impairments including learning disabilities, and mental illness (if recognised by a respected body of medical opinion).

Examples of conditions that are likely to be considered substantial include:

- inability to see moving traffic clearly enough to cross a road safely;

- inability to turn taps or knobs; and

- inability to remember and relay a simple message correctly.

Long-term effects can include:

- those which have lasted at least 12 months; or

- are likely to last at least 12 months; or

- are likely to last for the rest of the life of the person affected;

- those which are likely to recur: for instance an effect will be considered to be long term if it is likely both to recur, and to do so at least once beyond the 12-month period following the first occurrence.

Day-to-day activities are normal activities carried out by most people on a regular basis, and must involve one or more of the following categories:

- mobility - moving from place to place;

- manual dexterity - use of the hands and fingers;

- physical co-ordination;

- continence;

- the ability to lift, carry or move objects;

- speech, hearing or eyesight;

- memory, or ability to concentrate, learn or understand; and

- being able to recognise physical danger.

2.09 One of the first sections of the DDA already to have come into force, in July 1996, is Part II, on 'employment'. It is concerned with discrimination against both job applicants and employees; discrimination being defined as 'less favourable treatment'. The DDA requires employers to make all necessary adjustments to policies and procedures, and also to the physical features of premises, so that the disabled person concerned is not at 'a substantial disadvantage in comparison with persons who are not disabled'. A duty is placed upon employers, and prospective employers, 'to take such steps as are reasonable, in all the circumstances of the case'.

2.10 The Act gives examples of such steps:

- making adjustments to premises;

- allocating some of the disabled person's duties to another person;

- transferring them to fill an existing vacancy;

- altering their work hours;

- assigning them to a different place of work;

- allowing them to be absent during working hours for rehabilitation, assessment or treatment;

- giving them, or arranging for them to be given, training;

- acquiring or modifying equipment;

- modifying instructions or reference manuals;

- modifying procedures for testing or assessment;

- providing a reader or interpreter; and

- providing supervision.

2.11 With the implementation of the DDA the Government has also repealed the quota system provided for under the Disabled Persons (Employment) Act, 1974. Organizations with less than 15 employees are exempt from the new employment provisions set out in the DDA. Where employment discrimination is alleged disabled people have recourse to industrial tribunals. Part II came into force in November 1996, and already a substantial number of cases are being heard.

2.12 The provisions of the Act in relation to 'public transport' are also now being brought into effect and relate, in the main, to all kinds of 'vehicles', including ships, aircraft, trains, busses, trams, taxis and underground systems. Stations and inter-change points, however, will come within the scope of the provisions for premises by the end of 2004.

2.13 The provisions of the Act under Part IV in relation to 'education' came into force in November 1996. The new rights that the DDA gives to disabled people have effect in three main areas:

- employing staff. Employers, including governing bodies, LEAs, colleges of further education, and universities must not unjustifiably discriminate against current employees or job applicants on the grounds of disability, and may have to make reasonable adjustments to their employment arrangements and/ or premises if these substantially disadvantage a disabled person;

- providing non-educational services to the public. Governing bodies, LEAs, colleges of further education, and universities must not unjustifiably discriminate against disabled people when providing non-educational services. Examples might include the following:

  when letting rooms for community use; when putting on a school play or entertainment or fundraising event; when holding a reporting meeting for parents; when holding an exhibition of students' work; when holding an award ceremony, etc. From October 1999 they will be required to take reasonable steps to change policies, practices or procedures which make it impossible or unreasonably difficult for disabled people to use a service; provide auxiliary aids or services which would enable disabled people to use a service; and overcome physical barriers by providing a service by a reasonable alternative method. By the year 2004 they will have to take reasonable steps to remove, alter, or provide reasonable means of avoiding physical features that make it impossible or unreasonably difficult for a disabled person to use a service;

- publishing information about arrangements for disabled pupils and students. Governing bodies in their annual reports to parents must explain their admission arrangements for disabled pupils, how they will help such pupils gain access, and what they will do to make sure they are treated fairly. Colleges of further education and universities are required to make an annual return to the Audit Commission, setting out their current position in relation to the provisions of the DDA, and reporting the policies and measures which they have in hand to meet the Act's requirements.

2.14 Part III of the DDA, in force from October 1999, makes it unlawful on grounds of discrimination for providers of 'goods, facilities and services' (service providers) to discriminate against disabled people by:

- refusing service;

- providing a worse standard of service to disabled people than it provides to able bodied people; and

- offering service on worse terms.

Service providers will have to take reasonable steps to:

- change practices, policies or procedures which make it impossible or unreasonably difficult for disabled people to use a service (DDA, Section 21(1));

- overcome physical features which make it impossible or unreasonably difficult for disabled people to use the service, by providing the service by a reasonable alternative method (DDA, Section 21(2)(d)); and

- provide auxiliary aids or services which would make it easier for, or which, would enable disabled people to use a service (DDA, Section 21(4)).

2.15 From the end of 2004 service providers will have to take reasonable steps to remove, alter or provide reasonable means of avoiding physical features that make it impossible or unreasonably difficult for disabled people to use their services and facilities (DDA, Section 21(2)(a-c)).

2.16 It is under these provisions of the Act that it is likely that the 'reasonable steps' which will have to be taken will involve the alteration of the physical fabric of 'Premises'. It is important therefore to use the time available until 2005 to identify what physical features will have to be dealt with in this way, how to deal with them and at what stage before the end of 2004. This may also mean considering in which way a reasonable alternative method of making the service in question available to disabled persons can be provided. Planning for these circumstances should be undertaken as soon as possible so that alterations and reorganisation can be co-ordinated with, and carried out in conjunction with, planned maintenance programmes (see Section 3 and Appendix B).

2.17 'Facilities and Services' covered in the Act include the following:

- access to and use of any place which members of the public are permitted to enter;

- access to and use of means of communication;

- access to and use of information services; and

- facilities for entertainment, recreation or refreshment.

2.18 Implementation of Part III of the DDA will clearly be complex and will give rise to many issues of interpretation. These complexities, and the lead times needed for such sweeping changes, have meant that in the specific case of 'barriers' the Government provided a phasing-in period of ten years for their removal or elimination. However, where such barriers can be shown to be discriminatory in future in relation to the employment of an individual, or in relation to the provision of goods or services from October 1999 onwards, a barrier may need to be removed with the reasonable minimum of delay applicable in the circumstances. The judgement of the Court, or Tribunal will reflect whether all 'reasonable' steps have been taken to ensure that provision has been made for accessibility. It is of particular importance, therefore, to remember that while the DDA relates to the design of new and substantially extended buildings, as does Part M of the Building Regulations, perhaps more significantly it also relates to the refurbishment of buildings and the management and operation of existing premises and facilities. Given the very broad definitions contained in the Act, it now means that the relevant environmental standards arising from the application of the DDA extend considerably further than those set out in the Part M Approved Document.

2.19 With the implementation of the DDA it can be seen that it is vital to ensure that the overall and detailed design, and the specifications applicable to any new or altered building in public use, are carefully appraised in relation to the provisions of the Act. Only if this is done will the owners, operators and managers of new buildings minimise the real risk of having to alter their facility on its completion as the result of an action brought under the DDA. The **Accessibility Appraisal** of any building is therefore now a process which needs to be put in place during the early stages of project design and sustained throughout the whole of the following sequence of detailed/ construction design and specification.

2.20 In the context of the management and operation of existing premises, even including those that are newly completed, there is a need to carry out an Accessibility Audit. This is in order to be able, firstly to establish what conditions actually exist, and then, in the **Accessibility Audit Report**, to identify what steps can 'reasonably' be undertaken to eliminate discriminatory barriers. Indeed, until 2005, the view of the Courts or Tribunals in relation to many premises' issues may be that commissioning an Accessibility Audit, in itself constitutes sufficient 'reasonable' action, at least for an interim period, to avoid incurring any immediate penalty under the DDA.

2.21 Although implementation of the Act is still in its early stages it is clear that in the judgement of the Courts and Tribunals a number of factors will influence whether it is 'reasonable' for changes to be made. In particular these include:

- how much an alteration will improve the situation for disabled persons;

- how easy it is to make the changes;

- the cost of the measure, both financially and in terms of the disruption that it will cause;

- the building owner's resources; and

- financial help, or other help that may be available.

2.22 While building owners and facilities managers may well wish to make better provision for disabled people, perhaps in anticipation of the legal requirement to do so, some caution may need to be exercised. It has already been pointed out that the establishment of the 'Disability Rights Commission' is likely to lead to further expansion and strengthening of disability discrimination civil rights legislation. There have already been changes to Part M of the Building Regulations during 1999, and at least one further Code of Practice is due before 2004. The build up of cases will also give greater clarity to the interpretation of 'reasonableness'.

2.23 For further information about the DDA reference should be made to:

- HM Government
  Disability Discrimination Act 1995

- National Disability Council
  DDA Codes of Practice

  – Definitions

  – Employment

  – Rights of Access - Goods, Facilities Services and Premises

- DfEE: Department for Education and Employment
  What the Disability Discrimination Act (DDA) 1995 Means for Schools and LEAs.
  Circular number 3/97

  Access for Disabled People to School Buildings. Building Bulletin 91 (Spring 1999)

- DH: Department of Health

  *A Practical Guide for Disabled People - Where to Find Information, Services
  and Equipment*

  (Available also in Braille and audio-cassette) from:

  Department of Health
  PO Box 410
  Wetherby
  LS23 7LN

  All available from:

  The Stationery Office
  The Publications Centre
  PO Box 276
  London
  SW8 5DT

  General Enquiries: 0171 873 0011
  Tel (Orders): 0171 873 9090
  Fax (Orders): 0171 873 8200

3.00 ACCESSIBILITY APPRAISALS AND ACCESSIBILITY AUDITS

3.01 An Accessibility Appraisal/ Audit is not simply about getting wheelchairs in and out of an existing building. For an Accessibility Appraisal/ Audit to be effective it should embrace the needs of people with the whole spectrum of characteristics set out in Section 2. The process will involve a detailed appraisal of the design, or of the existing building, and its immediate surroundings. It will be prepared in consultation with the architect, or designer, and with the building's owners, operators and managers. It should, with benefit, also involve users.

3.02 Pro-forma documents for carrying out an Accessibility Appraisal/ Audit are illustrated in Appendix B. The documents are arranged in a sequence of 14 sheets covering the following:

Ref	Title	Sheet No.
A	Approach and car parking	01
B	Routes and external level change, including ramps and steps	02
C	Entrances, including reception	03/ 04
D	Horizontal movement and activities	05/ 06
E	Vertical movement and internal level change	07/ 08
F	Doors	09
G	Lavatories	10/ 11
H	Fixtures, fittings and equipment	12
J	Information and controls	13
K	Means of escape	14
S	Supplementary	S/ -
AN	Attached note	AN/ -

3.03 With the Accessibility Appraisal/ Audit Report as the base document building management strategies to achieve and sustain accessibility can be developed. Optimally this can be related to five-/ seven-year repair and maintenance cycles with prioritised items of expenditure allocated to successive years. It is helpful too if the Accessibility Appraisal/ Audit Report is supported by plans, diagrams and photographs where existing situations apply, as well as proposals for future implementation. It may well be that conflicts may arise between issues of security, safety and accessibility. The Accessibility Appraisal/ Audit Report should therefore be discussed with insurers and should stand alongside the building's fire safety and maintenance manuals.

3.04 The objectives in preparing the Accessibility (Appraisal/ Audit) Report should include:

- understanding how the building(s) and spaces between and around can best function, having in mind the needs of people with disabilities (Appraisal and Audit);

- agreeing operational access policies for them (Appraisal and Audit);

- agreeing procedures for variations to design proposals (Appraisal), or, establishing priorities, procedures and programmes for carrying out the works required (Audit);

- identifying the availability of resources, including finance (Appraisal and Audit);

- developing procedures for maintaining accessibility, safety and security, including during periods of construction, whether or not CDM Regulations apply (Appraisal and Audit); and

- developing procedures for subsequently maintaining the highest possible levels of accessibility on completion of the works (Appraisal and Audit).

3.05 Accessibility Design Appraisal: Format

Suggested format for an Accessibility Appraisal Report

Section 1 *Introduction*
General description of the building design and its arrangements, including any perceived challenges and issues relating to accessibility for people with disabilities as defined by the DDA.

Section 2 *Schedule*
A schedule of items prepared against use of the pro-formas commenting on all points needing attention.

Section 3 *Plans*
Plans (reduced) and diagrams, together with illustrations, and specifications of proposed items.

Section 4 *Conclusions*
Conclusions, including general observations, and recommendations.

Section 5 *Reference*
Sources of reference and design guidance, together with blank copies of the Appraisal assessment pro-formas.

(see example of layout of Section 2, Schedule)

Section 2, Schedule, suggested layout:

New Hospital

Disability Discrimination Act 1995: Accessibility Design Appraisal

Schedule of Comments / Observations on Loaded Design Plans

Drawing No
B 20 Z5412 P6

Level 2, Block 5, Loaded Plan

Space ref	Item ref	Comment
		(see also general comments in summary)
05.2.004		D, ES, 901 impedes wheelchair manoeuvre
05.2.005		no comment
05.2.006		no comment
05.2.007	WC/ SHWR (STAFF)	space is adequate for wheelchair use but layout is deficient: see summary comments (sheet 24); hand-basin does not relate well to WC pan; door should have capability to be opened outwards in emergency
05.2.008		signage locations not apparent
05.2.009	seating	waiting area leaves no space for wheelchairs/ buggies; no lowered section of reception counter is evident
05.2.010	WC (STAFF)	no comment
05.2.011/ 012/ 013		{ {no comment {
05.2.014	WC (STAFF)	Space is adequate for wheelchair use but layout is deficient: see summary comments (sheets 22 and 24); position of WC pan precludes independent transfer from/ to wheelchair; basin does not relate well to WC; door should have capability to open outwards in emergency
05.2.015	furniture	furniture impedes wheelchair manoeuvre CHA005 position precludes independent wheel-chair egress.
etc, etc		

3.06 Accessibility Audit Report: Format

Suggested format for an Accessibility Audit Report

Section 1 *Introduction*
General description of the building and its arrangements, including a summary of any perceived problems and issues relating to accessibility for people with disabilities as defined by the DDA.

Section 2 *Schedule*
A schedule of items extracted from the completed survey pro-formas listing and illustrating all points needing attention and indicating the possible action required together with its indicative cost and relative priority, following the sequence of the survey. The survey pro-formas follow the same sequence as the design guidance that follows (Design Guidance and Premises Management).

Section 3 *Photographs and diagrams*
Including plans (reduced), annotated with key relevant locations, together with illustrations and specifications of proposed items.

Section 4 *Conclusions*
Conclusions, including general observations and recommendations.

Section 5 *Reference*
Sources of reference and design guidance, together with blank copies of the Audit assessment pro-formas.

An example of the format which can be adopted is as follows:

Premises: School			
Item	**Action**	**Cost**	**Priority**
A. Approach			
A/1			
There is no designated disabled parking space in front of the school			
	Mark out two designated spaces as near to entrance door as possible + provide signs		
		£115	
		+ £40	
			next Fin. year
A/6			
Bollards are difficult to see in the dark			
	Provide reflective marker strips		
		8 x £20	
			routine maint.
etc, etc			

3.07 In arriving at the conclusions and recommendations of the Accessibility Audit Report it should be possible to place the proposals for action in the context of:

- day to day operating procedures;

- repair and maintenance programmes;

- minor works;

- adaptation and improvement works; and

- major works and whole building improvements,

Categories of prioritisation could be:

- *now*
  regarded as urgently needed, often to provide safe access as much as to achieve access itself.

- *routine maintenance*

  falling within routine procedures for maintenance and repair and perhaps requiring instruction and monitoring of suppliers and contractors (eg BT, towel suppliers, etc), and possibly staff.

- *next financial year*

  items to be included in the works programme of the first financial year available within the five-/ seven-year cycle. Items can be prioritised, and/ or identified by relative cost to achieve a satisfactory cash-flow situation, perhaps matched to fundraising throughout the whole five-/ seven-year cycle.

- *part of refurbishment*

  seen as needing to be included within proposals for the general refurbishment of the building.

If fundraising is necessary it may be helpful to group items together to show alternative proposals, offering a range of budget targets, perhaps related to different priorities.

3.08 Historic and 'Listed Buildings'

English Heritage's publication 'Easy Access to Historic Properties' quotes *Planning Policy Guidance Note 15: Planning and the Historic Environment*:

It is important in principle that disabled people should have dignified, easy access to and within historic buildings. If it is treated as part of an integrated review of access requirements for all users or visitors, and a flexible and pragmatic approach is taken, it should normally be possible to plan suitable access without compromising a building's special interest. Alternative routes or re-organising the use of spaces may achieve the desired result without the need for damaging alterations.

Taking the necessary steps towards satisfying these aims should result in the preparation of an 'Accessibility Plan'.

The key issues to be addressed within the plan will be the location and mode of entry to the building, circulation within it, and escape from it.

Other important issues include:

facility provision (lavatories, etc), signage, lighting and awareness training for staff.

To the above should be added: safety, security, and communications which will inevitably include establishing evacuation procedures for means of escape.

3.09 Accessibility Plans and Historic Fabric

The English Heritage Guidance proposes:

in devising an Access(ibility) Plan for an historic property, the key conservation principle should be minimum intervention in the historic fabric:

– measures which avoid or minimise the need for alteration should be considered first;

– alterations which adversely affect a property's special character should be avoided;

– alterations should form part of a long-term strategy for use;

– alterations should be reversible wherever possible.

3.10 Accessibility Plans - a flexible and pragmatic approach

The English Heritage Guidance, in advocating the development of Accessibility Plans, proposes that they should be based on a comprehensive assessment.

The assessment should:

- identify the existing physical and communication barriers to access (Accessibility Audit);

- examine the access needs of users (Accessibility Audit);

- assess the impact of these on features of historic, architectural or archaeological interest, and/ or their setting; and

- devise solutions which reconcile access and conservation needs (Accessibility Plan).

3.11 Accessibility Plans and Reversibility

The Guidance goes on to say:

Reversibility should not be used to justify solutions of an insensitive or inappropriately ephemeral nature. In some cases, permanent, high-quality intervention in a building's fabric may offer a more satisfactory solution in terms of preserving its special architectural or historic interest, especially where overall architectural coherence is a more important criterion than the sensitivity of the building fabric. Under certain circumstances the use of a separate form or structure detached from the historic building and designed in a modern idiom may also be appropriate.

4.00 DESIGN GUIDANCE, AND PREMISES MANAGEMENT

A   Approach and car parking

4.01 Approach routes to any premises should be distinctively sign-posted and there should be clearly indicated and signed car parking provision for disabled drivers. Control gates or barriers should not form an impediment to disabled drivers. The principal entrance should be obvious to those approaching, with one route for all, and both the disabled parking and the setting down point should be as close to it as possible. If possible, shelter should be provided at the setting down point. The approach should be well lit and surfaced with material that does not impede movement, is well maintained and slip-resistant, and helps to inform about direction of movement.

4.02 To achieve these objectives:

- signage should use upper and lower case letters and colour/ tone contrast;

- disabled parking bays should be sign-posted and apparent as the building is approached;

- parking bays should be wide and long enough to allow car doors, tail-gates and boot lids to be fully opened and transfer to and from a wheelchair effected;

- kerbs should be dropped between setting down points and/ or disabled parking bays and the approach to the principal building entrance;

- where there are existing loose surfaces a smooth 'pathway' of paviors should be inset. This should also be done where disabled drivers alight from their vehicles; and

- the approach should be kept clear of ice, snow and fallen leaves.

Sources

- *Building Regulations 1992, Part M Approved Document*

- *Designing for Accessibility (CAE)*

- *Buildings for All to Use (CIRIA)*

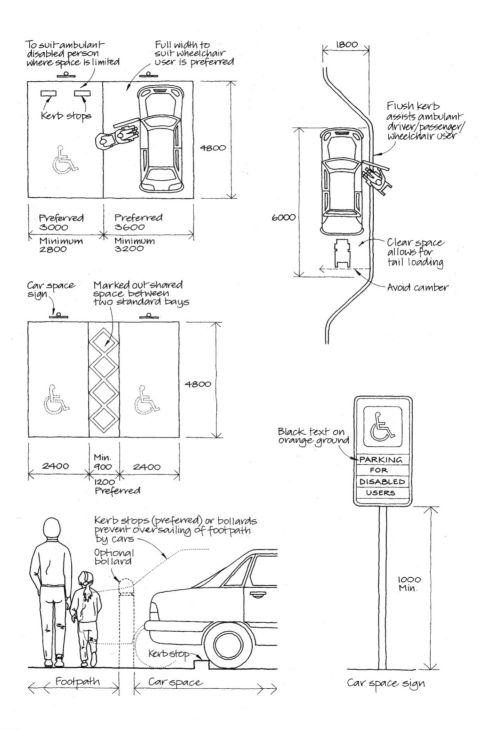

To suit ambulant disabled person where space is limited

Full width to suit wheelchair user is preferred

Kerb stops

1800

Flush kerb assists ambulant driver/passenger/wheelchair user

4800

6000

Preferred 3000

Preferred 3600

Minimum 2800

Minimum 3200

Clear space allows for tail loading

Avoid camber

Car space sign

Marked out shared space between two standard bays

4800

2400

Min. 900

2400

1200 Preferred

Black text on orange ground

PARKING FOR DISABLED USERS

1000 Min.

Kerb stops (preferred) or bollards prevent oversailing of footpath by cars

Optional bollard

Kerb stop

Footpath

Car space

Car space sign

FIG 1

32

B Routes and external level change, including ramps and steps

4.03 External routes and level changes should seek to minimise the effects of gradient, while any ramped surface should be clearly indicated. Surfaces should be slip-resistant and where ramped should have kerbs, and offer the alternative of steps with step nosings clearly marked and with handrails where appropriate. Routes should be clearly sign-posted, well lit and free of unmarked obstructions such as branches, projecting windows or signs giving rise to clashes at head height.

4.04 To achieve these objectives:

- paths should preferably be at least 1,800mm wide, or 1,500mm minimum with passing spaces, and should have defined edges;

- ramps should not be steeper than 1:12 pitch with 5m maximum length; ramps at 1:15 pitch, or shallower are preferred, not exceeding 10m in length without level intermediate resting places. All ramps should have level platforms at top and bottom;

- ramp surfaces should be slip-resistant and there should be kerbs and handrails provided wherever possible;

- there should preferably be steps as an alternative to any ramp, with consistent treads and risers, and contrasting nosings and handrails which extend at least 300mm beyond the top and bottom steps;

- routes should be clearly lit, with particular attention paid to ramps and steps. Handrails should contrast with their background;

- where a permanent ramp can not be provided, perhaps because the building is Listed, a temporary ramp may be an acceptable alternative;

- very long ramps should be avoided and powered external means of vertical movement considered when height exceeds 1,200mm (see E); and

- planting can provide valuable cues and orientation information, particularly for people with visual disabilities, but will need to be maintained.

Sources

- *Building Regulations 1992, Part M Approved Document*

- *Designing for Accessibility (CAE)*

- *Buildings for All to Use (CIRIA)*

- *Easy Access to Historic Properties (English Heritage)*

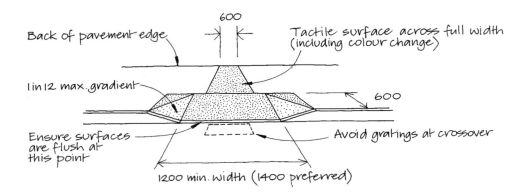

Back of pavement edge

600

Tactile surface across full width (including colour change)

1 in 12 max. gradient

600

Ensure surfaces are flush at this point

Avoid gratings at crossover

1200 min. width (1400 preferred)

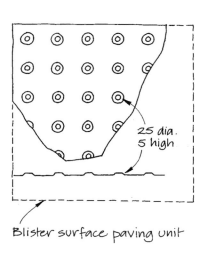

25 dia. 5 high

Blister surface paving unit

FIG 2

34

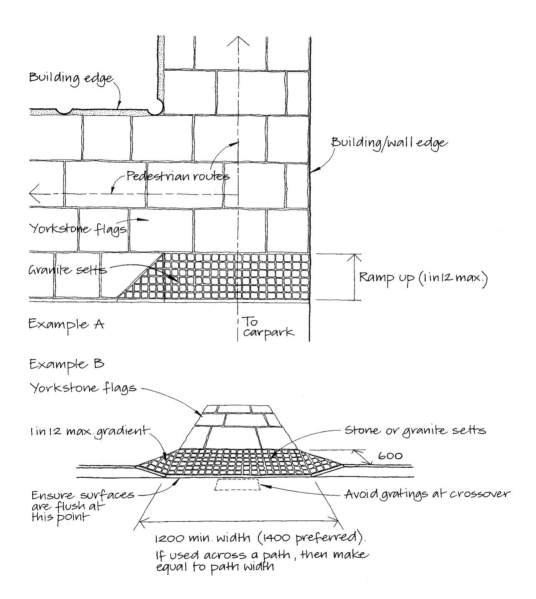

Building edge

Building/wall edge

Pedestrian routes

Yorkstone flags

Granite setts

Ramp up (1 in 12 max.)

Example A

To carpark

Example B

Yorkstone flags

1 in 12 max. gradient

Stone or granite setts

600

Ensure surfaces are flush at this point

Avoid gratings at crossover

1200 min. width (1400 preferred).
If used across a path, then make
equal to path width

Textured drop kerb warning

FIG 3

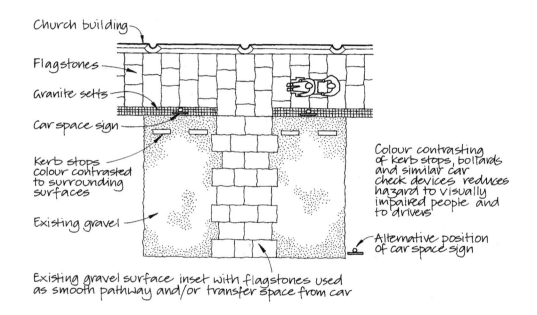

Church building

Flagstones

Granite setts

Car space sign

Kerb stops
colour contrasted
to surrounding
surfaces

Existing gravel

Colour contrasting
of kerb stops, bollards
and similar car
check devices reduces
hazard to visually
impaired people and
to drivers

Alternative position
of car space sign

Existing gravel surface inset with flagstones used
as smooth pathway and/or transfer space from car

FIG 4

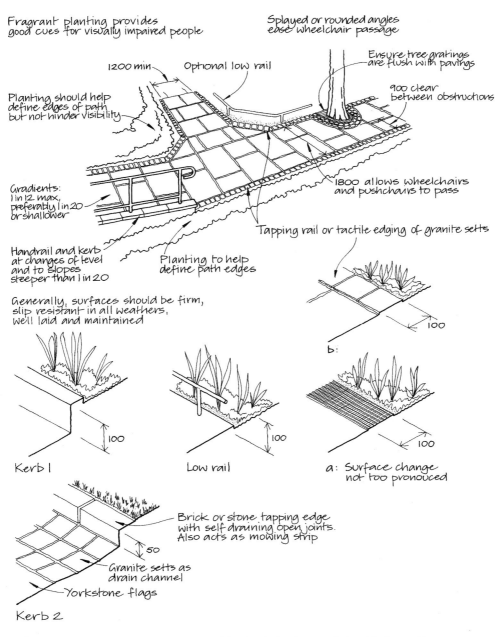

Fragrant planting provides good cues for visually impaired people

Splayed or rounded angles ease wheelchair passage

1200 min

Optional low rail

Ensure tree gratings are flush with pavings

900 clear between obstructions

Planting should help define edges of path but not hinder visibility

Gradients:
1 in 12 max,
preferably 1 in 20
or shallower

Handrail and kerb at changes of level and to slopes steeper than 1 in 20

Planting to help define path edges

1800 allows wheelchairs and pushchairs to pass

Tapping rail or tactile edging of granite setts

Generally, surfaces should be firm, slip resistant in all weathers, well laid and maintained

b:

100

100

100

100

Kerb 1

Low rail

a: Surface change not too pronounced

Brick or stone tapping edge with self draining open joints. Also acts as mowing strip

50

Granite setts as drain channel

Yorkstone flags

Kerb 2

Tactile routes   Edges defined for both tactile and visual information

FIG 5

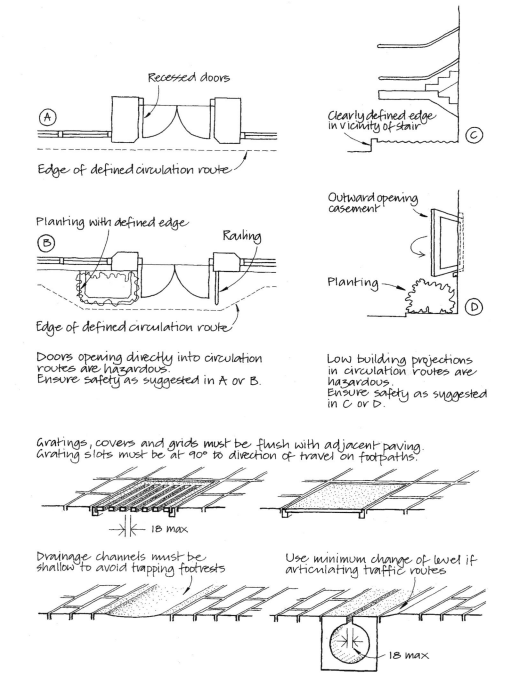

Recessed doors

(A)

Edge of defined circulation route

Planting with defined edge

Railing

(B)

Edge of defined circulation route

Doors opening directly into circulation routes are hazardous.
Ensure safety as suggested in A or B.

Clearly defined edge in vicinity of stair

(C)

Outward opening casement

Planting

(D)

Low building projections in circulation routes are hazardous.
Ensure safety as suggested in C or D.

Gratings, covers and grids must be flush with adjacent paving.
Grating slots must be at 90° to direction of travel on footpaths.

18 max

Drainage channels must be shallow to avoid trapping footrests

Use minimum change of level if articulating traffic routes

18 max

FIG 6

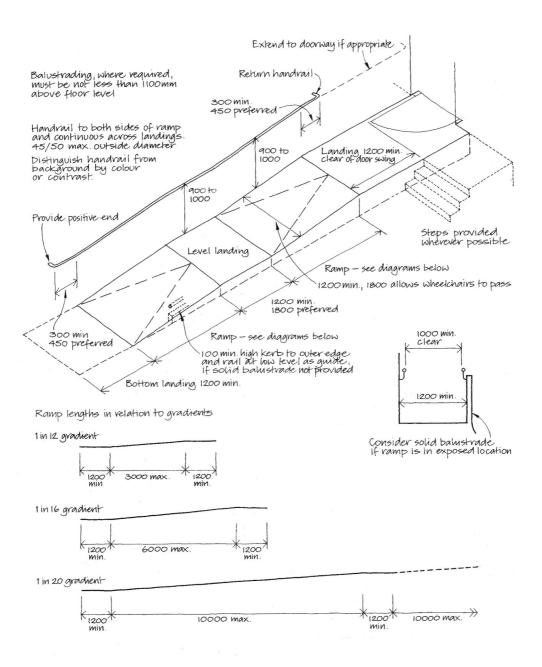

Extend to doorway if appropriate

Balustrading, where required, must be not less than 1100mm above floor level

Return handrail

300 min. 450 preferred

Handrail to both sides of ramp and continuous across landings. 45/50 max. outside diameter

Distinguish handrail from background by colour or contrast.

900 to 1000

Landing 1200 min. clear of door swing

900 to 1000

Provide positive end

Level landing

Steps provided wherever possible

Ramp — see diagrams below

1200 min., 1800 allows wheelchairs to pass

1200 min. 1800 preferred

300 min 450 preferred

Ramp — see diagrams below

100 min. high kerb to outer edge and rail at low level as guide, if solid balustrade not provided

Bottom landing 1200 min.

1000 min. clear

1200 min.

Consider solid balustrade if ramp is in exposed location

Ramp lengths in relation to gradients

1 in 12 gradient

1200 min   3000 max.   1200 min.

1 in 16 gradient

1200 min.   6000 max.   1200 min.

1 in 20 gradient

1200 min.   10000 max.   1200 min.   10000 max.

FIG 7

39

B

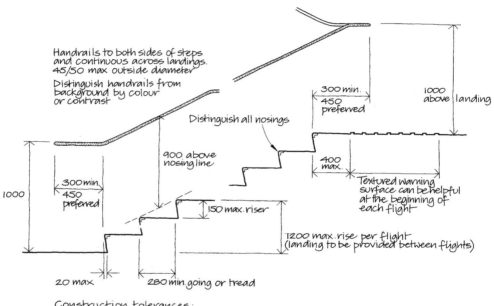

Handrails to both sides of steps
and continuous across landings.
45/50 max outside diameter

Distinguish handrails from
background by colour
or contrast

Distinguish all nosings

300 min.
450
preferred

1000
above landing

900 above
nosing line

400
max.

300 min.
450
preferred

Textured warning
surface can be helpful
at the beginning of
each flight

1000

150 max. riser

1200 max. rise per flight
(landing to be provided between flights)

20 max

280 min. going or tread

Construction tolerances:
± 3 on risers
± 5 on treads

Balustrades, where required, must be not less than 1100 above
floor, flight or landing levels

FIG 8

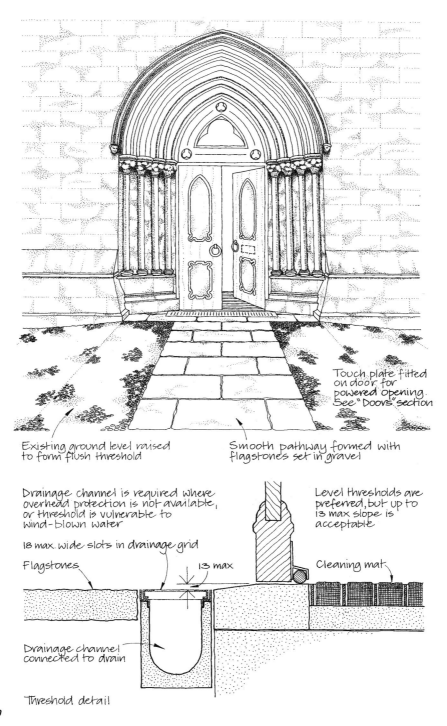

Touch plate fitted on door for powered opening. See "Doors" section

Existing ground level raised to form flush threshold

Smooth pathway formed with flagstones set in gravel

Drainage channel is required where overhead protection is not available, or threshold is vulnerable to wind-blown water

Level thresholds are preferred, but up to 13 max slope is acceptable

18 max. wide slots in drainage grid

Flagstones

13 max

Cleaning mat

Drainage channel connected to drain

Threshold detail

FIG 9

C   Entrances, including reception

4.05 The principal entrance should be 'for everyone', and should be easily distinguished, and welcoming. At the point of entry access should be level. Lobbies should be big enough for manoeuvre by people using pushchairs and wheelchairs, with outer and inner doors openable independently from a wheelchair. Floor surfaces at the point of entry should not impede movement, and glazing to lobbies and doors should avoid the risk of clashes or collisions. Access to the building will need to be reconciled with security requirements. On entering the building the reception point should be obvious and communication should be possible at both standing and seated heights. Staff should be appropriately trained. Information about the layout of the building should be apparent. The reception point is usually an appropriate location for a publicly usable telephone which should be suitable for use from a wheelchair and by a person with a hearing disability.

4.06 To achieve these objectives:

- principal entrances should be accessible, clearly sign-posted and well lit;

- substantially glazed entrances and entrance doors should be clearly marked at both standing and seated eye levels to provide for both safety and visibility;

- door furniture should be easy to grip and operate, and the force required to overcome the power of a door-closing mechanism should be kept to the minimum, compatible with its function, including weather exclusion;

- thresholds should be flush, and, if possible, absolutely level. Mats in mat-wells and other shoe and wheel cleaning surfaces should also be firmly fixed, flush and level, avoiding tripping hazards;

- power-operated automatic doors may be appropriate in some circumstances where doors have heavy traffic and both accessibility and energy conservation are considerations. Automatic doors that swing towards the user can be hazardous and should be appropriately signed. Automatic doors should stand open long enough for a slow moving person to pass through;

- lobbies should have dimensions which allow wheelchair users to move clear of the first door before opening the second;

- the entrance should offer a transition zone where people with sight disabilities can adjust from a bright exterior to an interior with subdued lighting;

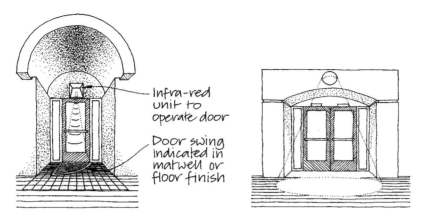

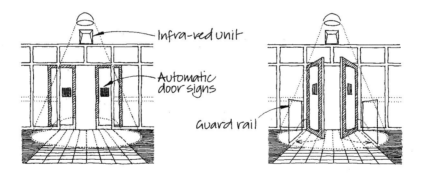

C

Infra-red
unit to
operate door

Door swing
indicated in
matwell or
floor finish

Entrances must be easily distinguishable from the facade,
using colour, detail, lighting and texture.
They should also relate safely and logically to circulation
routes

Infra-red unit

Automatic
door signs

Guard rail

The approach to automatic opening doors must be well defined,
using tactile and visual information.
Hinged doors, if not properly safeguarded, present a hazard to
people approaching them.

FIG 10

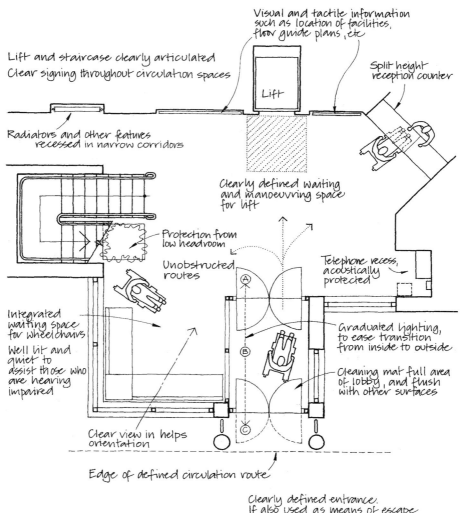

Visual and tactile information such as location of facilities, floor guide plans, etc.

Lift and staircase clearly articulated
Clear signing throughout circulation spaces

Split height reception counter

Lift

Radiators and other features recessed in narrow corridors

Clearly defined waiting and manoeuvring space for lift

Protection from low headroom

Unobstructed routes

Telephone recess, acoustically protected

Integrated waiting space for wheelchairs

Well lit and quiet to assist those who are hearing impaired

Graduated lighting, to ease transition from inside to outside

Cleaning mat full area of lobby, and flush with other surfaces

Clear view in helps orientation

Edge of defined circulation route

Clearly defined entrance. If also used as means of escape then door must open out.

FIG 11

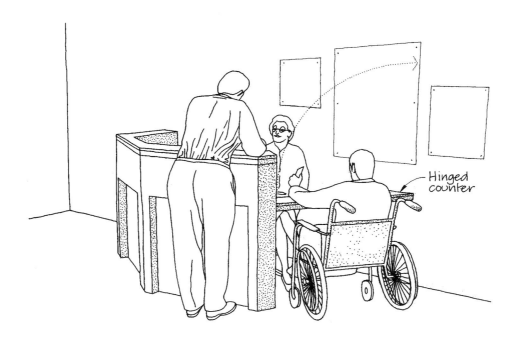

Hinged counter

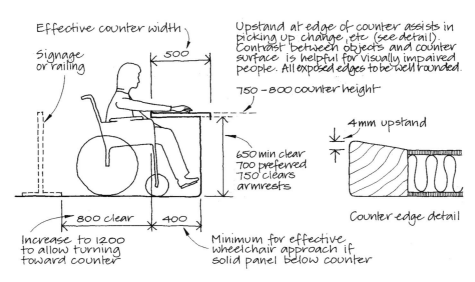

Effective counter width

Signage or railing

500

Upstand at edge of counter assists in picking up change, etc (see detail). Contrast between objects and counter surface is helpful for visually impaired people. All exposed edges to be well rounded.

750 – 800 counter height

4mm upstand

650 min clear
700 preferred
750 clears armrests

800 clear   400

Counter edge detail

Increase to 1200 to allow turning toward counter

Minimum for effective wheelchair approach if solid panel below counter

Reception counter/bookstall counter accessible to wheelchair user

FIG 12

- any reception point/ information hatch should have a lowered section of the counter with a flat surface usable from a wheelchair, it should be well lit and provide hearing assistance;

- waiting areas at reception should have seating and space for wheelchair users;

- signage should be in upper and lower case with contrasting colour/ tone; and

- any public telephone should be usable from a wheelchair with an adjacent shelf for writing on, well lit instructions readable from seated eye level and hearing aid coupling.

Sources

- *Building Regulations 1992, Part M Approved Document*

- *Designing for Accessibility (CAE)*

- *Buildings for All to Use (CIRIA)*

- *Easy Access to Historic Properties (English Heritage)*

D   Horizontal movement and activities (see also section F: Doors)

4.07 Movement at each level should be unimpeded and unobstructed. Corridors and activity spaces should permit independent wheelchair manoeuvre and movement by people with visual disabilities. The use of colour, texture, lighting and signage can all contribute to the clarity with which the building can be comprehended and its component parts identified. Lighting should avoid glare and silhouetting. Teaching and training areas should be equipped to provide hearing assistance.

D

4.08 To achieve these objectives:

- ideally 1,800mm should be allowed for wheelchairs to pass each other;

- minimum corridor width should be 1,200mm, but if narrower passages can not be avoided doors into spaces off should have at least 1,000mm doorsets;

- turning circles for wheelchair users should be not less than 1,500mm;

- any lobby should be sized to enable a wheelchair user to move clear of the first door and its swing before negotiating the second;

- door closer pressure should be kept to a minimum;

- where double doors are required in any corridor one leaf should always provide a minimum clear opening of 750mm;

- natural lighting should avoid glare and silhouetting;

- artificial lighting should avoid glare;

- communication spaces should have the capability for the provision of hearing assistance and should have an acoustic environment that minimises sound reverberation and reflection;

- colour/ tone contrasted, upper and lower case signage, and tactile information systems should be provided wherever possible;

- excessive monochromatic colour schemes should be avoided and floor and wall surfaces should be contrasted;

- develop, maintain and monitor environmental management systems where appropriate. The role of staff training in ensuring that communications with people with disabilities are effective should be recognised; and

Minimum approach requirements

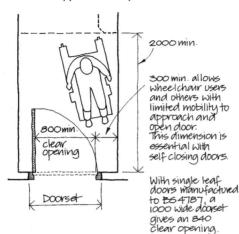

2000 min.

300 min. allows wheelchair users and others with limited mobility to approach and open door. This dimension is essential with self closing doors.

800 min. clear opening

Doorset

With single leaf doors manufactured to BS 4787, a 1000 wide doorset gives an 840 clear opening.

Door variations

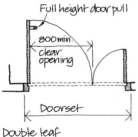

Full height door pull

800 min. clear opening

Doorset

Double leaf

Full height door pulls and large weatherboards may restrict usefulness of clear opening.

With double leaf doors a 1800 wide doorset gives an 810 clear opening to each leaf. Less than 1800 will result in unequal leaves if an 800 min. clear opening to one leaf is to be maintained (shown).

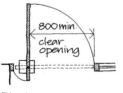

800 min. clear opening

Pivot

800 min. clear opening

Sliding

Exit Doors:

A level threshold is required, and an external ramp if necessary.

Lobby variations

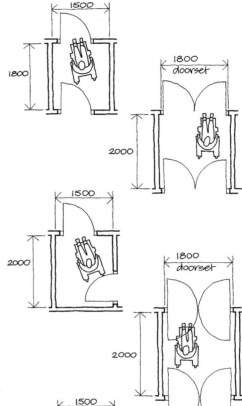

1500

1800

1800 doorset

2000

1500

2000

1800 doorset

2000

1500

2400

Layout of Lobbies:

The layout of lobbies will be determined by –
a) door location and the direction of swing.
b) the need of wheelchair users and others with limited mobility to pass clear of one door before approaching and opening the second door.

FIG 13

Dimensions and shaded areas provide the minimum space required for users of standard wheelchairs to approach and turn through doorways

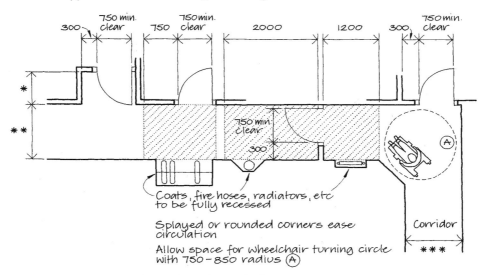

300   750 min. clear   750   750 min. clear   2000   1200   300   750 min. clear

750 min. clear

300

Coats, fire hoses, radiators, etc to be fully recessed

Splayed or rounded corners ease circulation

Allow space for wheelchair turning circle with 750 – 850 radius Ⓐ

Corridor
***

* Recess not less than width of door leaf. Hazardous if door opens into confined circulation route

** For corridors greater than 1200 wide 900 wide doorsets can be used
For corridors less than 1200 wide 1000 wide doorsets must be used

*** Aisles and corridors 1800 wide will allow wheelchairs to pass

Internal Lobbies:
Generally, requirements are similar to those for entrance lobbies.
X : Nominal 100, from hinge to wall. Allows door to open more than 90°, which eases turning of wheelchair through doorway
Y : 1200 minimum

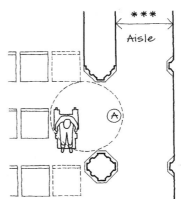

***
Aisle

Minimum space required for wheelchair user to be with companion if reserved positions further forward are temporarily unavailable

See also "Fixtures and Fittings" section for sightlines and visibility

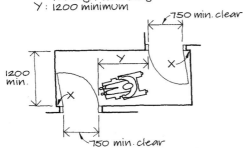

750 min. clear

1200 min.

X

X

750 min. clear

FIG 14

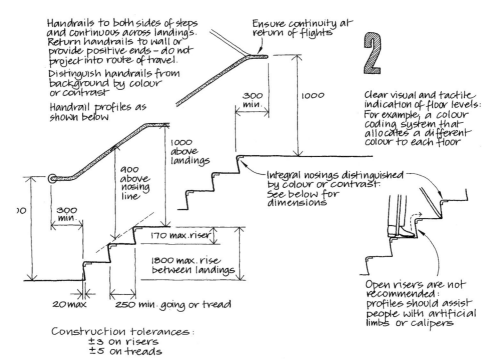

Handrails to both sides of steps
and continuous across landings.
Return handrails to wall or
provide positive ends – do not
project into route of travel.

Ensure continuity at
return of flights

2

Distinguish handrails from
background by colour
or contrast

Clear visual and tactile
indication of floor levels:
For example, a colour
coding system that
allocates a different
colour to each floor

Handrail profiles as
shown below

1000

300
min.

1000
above
landings

900
above
nosing
line

Integral nosings distinguished
by colour or contrast.
See below for
dimensions

)0

300
min.

170 max. riser

1800 max. rise
between landings

Open risers are not
recommended:
profiles should assist
people with artificial
limbs or calipers

20 max   250 min. going or tread

Construction tolerances:
±3 on risers
±5 on treads

Balustrades, where required, must be not less than 1100 above floor, flight
or landing levels

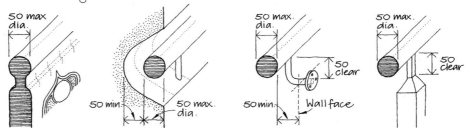

50 max.
dia.

50 max.
dia.

50 max.
dia.

50 max.
dia.

50 min.   50 max.
dia.

50
clear

50
clear

50 min.   Wall face

Handrail profiles should provide adequate grip and support at all times

Ensure a 1000 min. clearance is maintained between handrails on flights
and landings.
If a flight is more than 1800 wide
it must be divided, preferably with
a double handrail, 100 min. apart

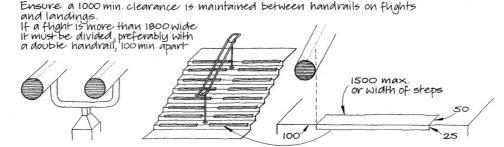

1500 max.
or width of steps

50

100   25

FIG 15

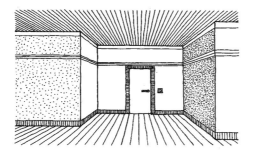

Use visual contrast to distinguish floor, wall and ceiling planes, door surrounds, decorative features

Light from side gives good modelling and definition to subjects

Try to avoid silhouetting in circulation and meeting areas

FIG 16

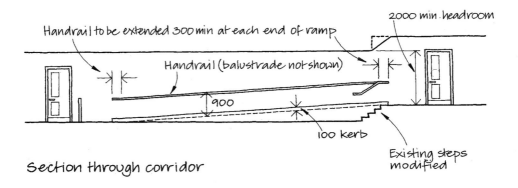

Handrail to be extended 300 min at each end of ramp

Handrail (balustrade not shown)

2000 min headroom

900

100 kerb

Existing steps modified

Section through corridor

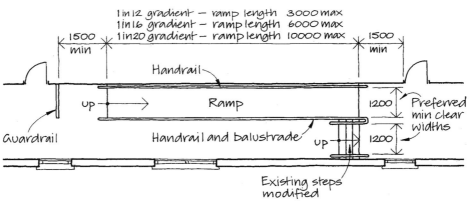

1 in 12 gradient — ramp length 3000 max
1 in 16 gradient — ramp length 6000 max
1 in 20 gradient — ramp length 10000 max

1500 min

1500 min

Handrail

Up →

Ramp

1200

Preferred min clear widths

Guardrail

Handrail and balustrade

Up

1200

Existing steps modified

Plan of corridor

Where width of corridor makes this layout impracticable a full width ramp may be preferred

Ramped adaptation to existing corridor steps

FIG 17

- issues of health and safety, security, and means of escape should all be addressed and co-ordinated. Items such as fire hose-reels and extinguishers should be positioned/ recessed to be clearly visible but not obstruct or create hazards for visually disabled people.

Sources

- *Building Regulations 1992, Part M Approved Document*

- *Designing for Accessibility (CAE)*

- *Buildings for All to Use (CIRIA)*

- *Easy Access to Historic Properties (English Heritage)*

- *What the Disability Discrimination Act (DDA) 1995 Means for Schools and LEAs (DfEE circular number 3/97)*

- *DfEE Constructional Standards 1997*

D

E   **Vertical movement and internal level change (see also B: Ramps)**

4.09 Stairs and ramps are the most common way of achieving change of level within a building, but lifts, short-rise platform lifts and stair-lifts may also offer the scope for level change, particularly where a gain (or loss) of height will exceed 1,200mm, but be less than a full storey in height. All internal changes of level, including single steps or ramps should be clearly indicated. Where ramps are provided the pitch, or gradient, should be acceptable for people with disabilities and steps should be provided as an alternative wherever possible. The pitch of all steps and ramps should be consistent. Where powered means of changing level is provided it should be clearly sign-posted, have operational instructions that are clear for people with all kinds of disabilities, comply with all relevant Codes of Practice and Regulations in relation to safety, be regularly maintained and its operation monitored.

4.10 To achieve these objectives:

- provide colour/ tone/ texture/ contrast/ lighting indicators, and handrails, where appropriate, at all changes of level;

- establish tolerances for the dimensions of treads and risers to all sequences of steps and stairs, and of ramp gradients;

- ensure that all stair nosings are clearly marked in contrast with the treads and risers;

- in the case of any passenger lift:

  – provide unobstructed space, 1,500 x 1,500mm minimum in front of the doors at each landing and 1,100 x 1,400mm within the car;

  – ensure that controls at the point of call and within the lift car are within reach and are clearly visible from both standing and seated height; not less than 900mm and not more than1,200mm above floor;

  – lift doors should have a clear opening width of 800mm and remain open for an adequate time to allow entry; sensor devices should ensure that doors do not close on a slow user or wheelchair;

  – audible announcements and visual displays will help people with sensory disabilities;

  – raised numbers beside control buttons will help people with sight impairments; Braille is read only by a small number of visually disabled people;

  – lift cars preferably should have an emergency telephone, which should have an inductive coupler for hearing-aid users;

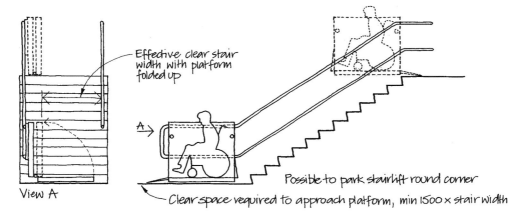

Effective clear stair width with platform folded up

View A

A→

Possible to park stairlift round corner

Clear space required to approach platform, min 1500 x stair width

Wheelchair stairlift gives access between storeys.
Support rails mounted on balustrades or adjacent walls.
Installations can suit straight flights, landings or curved stairs.
Controls and drive motor can be integral with platform or remotely sited.

FIG 18

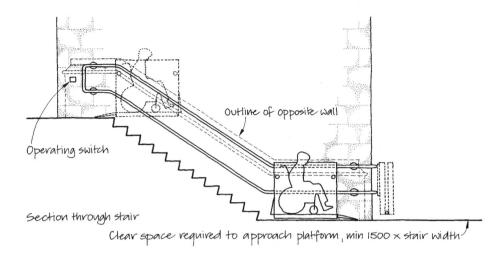

Operating switch

Outline of opposite wall

Section through stair

Clear space required to approach platform, min 1500 x stair width

Support rails mounted on balustrades or adjacent walls.
Installations can suit straight flights, landings or curved stairs.
Controls and drive motor can be integral with platform or remotely sited.

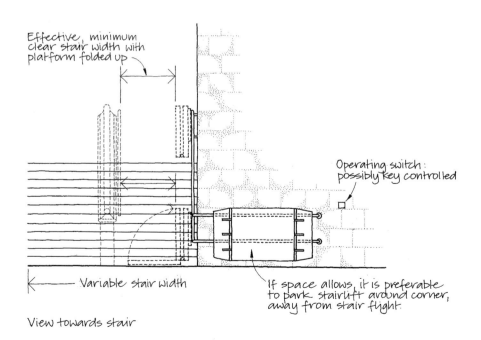

Effective, minimum clear stair width with platform folded up

Operating switch: possibly key controlled

Variable stair width

If space allows, it is preferable to park stairlift around corner, away from stair flight.

View towards stair

FIG 19

56

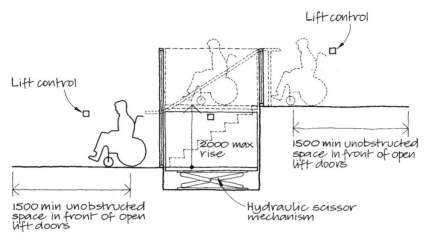

Lift control

Lift control

2000 max rise

1500 min unobstructed space in front of open lift doors

1500 min unobstructed space in front of open lift doors

Hydraulic scissor mechanism

Section through lift

Minimum internal dimensions:
1000 wide × 1200 long

View of lift

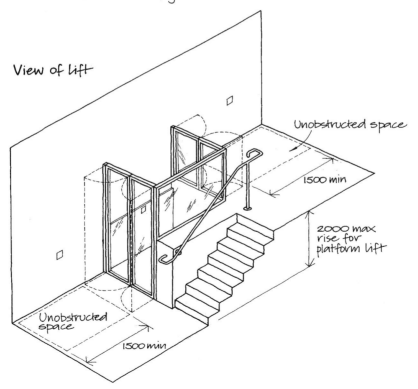

Unobstructed space

1500 min

2000 max rise for platform lift

Unobstructed space

1500 min

FIG 20

E

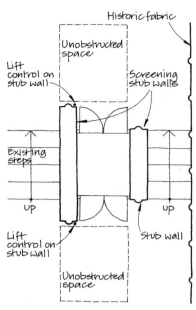

Historic fabric

Unobstructed space

Lift control on stub wall

Screening stub walls

Existing steps

UP

Lift control on stub wall

Stub wall

Unobstructed space

Plan of lift (see "View")
This arrangement gives protection to historic fabric, leaving it undisturbed

Options in relation to steps

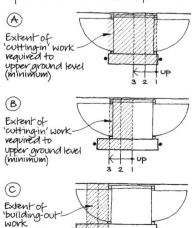

(A) Extent of 'cutting-in' work required to upper ground level (minimum)

3 2 1 UP

(B) Extent of 'cutting-in' work required to upper ground level (minimum)

3 2 1 UP

(C) Extent of 'building-out' work required to upper ground level (minimum)

3 2 1 UP

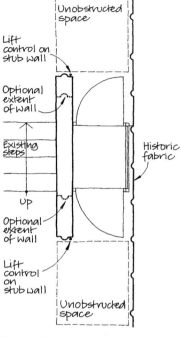

Unobstructed space

Lift control on stub wall

Optional extent of wall

Existing steps

UP

Historic fabric

Optional extent of wall

Lift control on stub wall

Unobstructed space

Alternative plan arrangement with lift adjacent to historic fabric.
Single door lift example shown

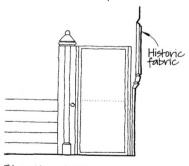

Historic fabric

Elevation of lift

FIG 21

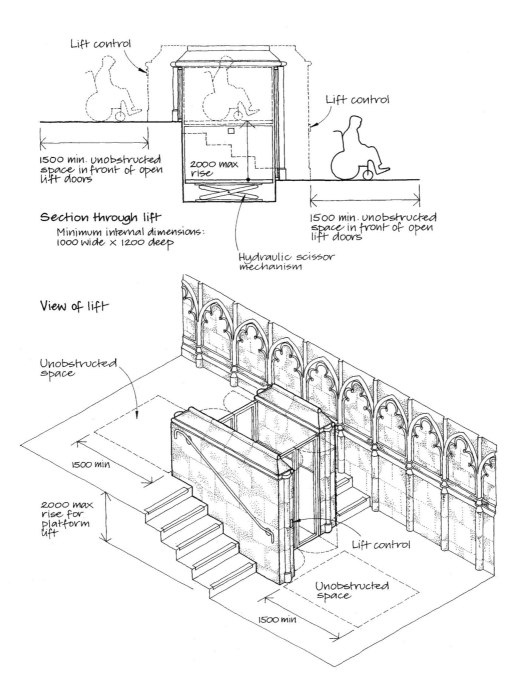

Lift control

1500 min. unobstructed space in front of open lift doors

Lift control

2000 max rise

1500 min. unobstructed space in front of open lift doors

Section through lift

Minimum internal dimensions: 1000 wide × 1200 deep

Hydraulic scissor mechanism

View of lift

Unobstructed space

1500 min

2000 max rise for platform lift

Lift control

Unobstructed space

1500 min

E

FIG 22

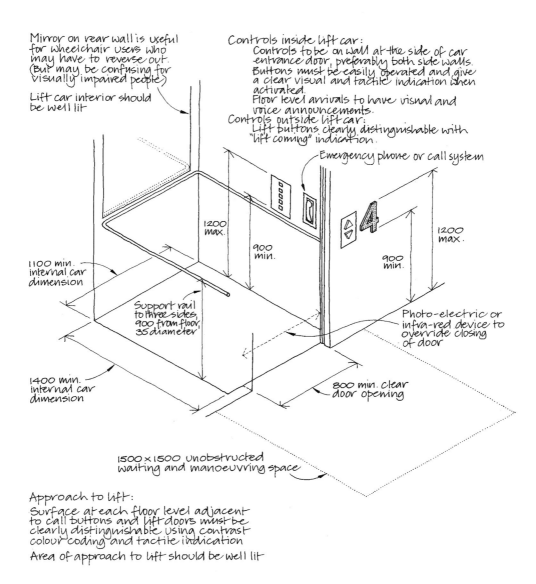

Mirror on rear wall is useful for wheelchair users who may have to reverse out. (But may be confusing for visually impaired people)

Lift car interior should be well lit

Controls inside lift car:
Controls to be on wall at the side of car entrance door, preferably both side walls.
Buttons must be easily operated and give a clear visual and tactile indication when activated.
Floor level arrivals to have visual and voice announcements.

Controls outside lift car:
Lift buttons clearly distinguishable with "lift coming" indication.

Emergency phone or call system

1200 max.

900 min.

1100 min. internal car dimension

Support rail to three sides, 900 from floor, 35 diameter

1400 min. internal car dimension

1200 max.

900 min.

Photo-electric or infra-red device to override closing of door

800 min. clear door opening

1500 × 1500 unobstructed waiting and manoeuvring space

Approach to lift:
Surface at each floor level adjacent to call buttons and lift doors must be clearly distinguishable using contrast colour coding and tactile indication

Area of approach to lift should be well lit

FIG 23

– any alarm button in a lift car should be fitted with a visual acknowledgement that the alarm bell has sounded for those lift users unable to hear it.

- in the case of any platform lift:

  – it should be clearly signposted;

  – it should have key/ security controlled operation; and

  – there should be adjacent stairs.

- in the case of any platform stairlift:

  – ensure that it does not compromise means of escape;

  – parking should be programmed to avoid obstruction; and

  – it should have key/ security controlled operation.

- in the case of all powered means of level change ensure that installation, operation, regular inspection and maintenance are carried out correctly and supervised by suitably trained personnel.

Sources

- *Building Regulations 1992, Part M Approved Document*

- *Designing for Accessibility (CAE)*

- *Buildings for All to Use (CIRIA)*

- *Easy Access to Historic Properties (English Heritage)*

- *Wheelchair Stairlifts and Platform Lifts (CAE)*

E

F   Doors

4.11 Doors are intended both to give access to and to enclose spaces. It is all too easy, however, for badly designed doors to become barriers. It is important therefore that all doors/ doorways/ access to stairs do not present obstacles to disabled people. Fire doors in particular can be an impediment and the opportunity for them to be held open by alarm-linked devices should be taken whenever possible. All door furniture should be able to be operated with ease, even by people with limited dexterity and power. It is also extremely important that there is optimum visibility for those approaching a door from either side of it.

4.12 To achieve these objectives:

- doors should be eliminated where possible;

- where doors are necessary colour contrast should be used to help distinguish the door frame from its surroundings;

- door furniture should be easily gripped and operated, clearly visible, and contrasted against its background;

- door closer force should be kept to a minimum;

- alarm-linked hold-back devices on fire doors should be used wherever possible;

- visibility panels should be provided, related to both standing and seated eye levels, whenever possible;

- where double doors are necessary one leaf should always provide a minimum clear opening of 750mm even if that requires unequal leaves, rather than oblige a wheelchair to open both parts of the door; and

- it is vitally important that there should be sufficient manoeuvre space on the opening side of any door, but especially when a door is self-closing into a corner.

Sources

- *Building Regulations 1992, Part M Approved Document*

- *Designing for Accessibility (CAE)*

- *Buildings for All to Use (CIRIA)*

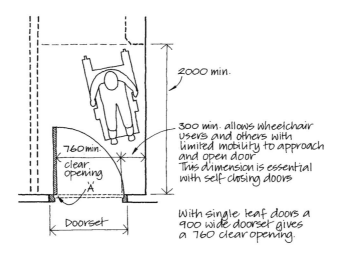

2000 min.

300 min. allows wheelchair users and others with limited mobility to approach and open door
This dimension is essential with self-closing doors

760 min. clear opening 'A'

Doorset

With single leaf doors a 900 wide doorset gives a 760 clear opening.

Door variation

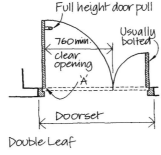

Full height door pull

760 min. clear opening 'A'

Usually bolted

Doorset

Double Leaf

Full height door pulls may restrict usefulness of clear opening

With double leaf doors an 1800 wide doorset gives an 810 clear opening to each leaf.
Less than 1800 will result in unequal leaves if a 760 min clear opening to one leaf is to be maintained (shown)

Door edge detail at 'A'

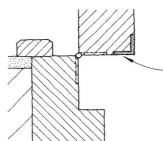

Door edge is at maximum risk of damage from wheelchair hub

Protective metal angle let into door edge can be helpful.

FIG 24

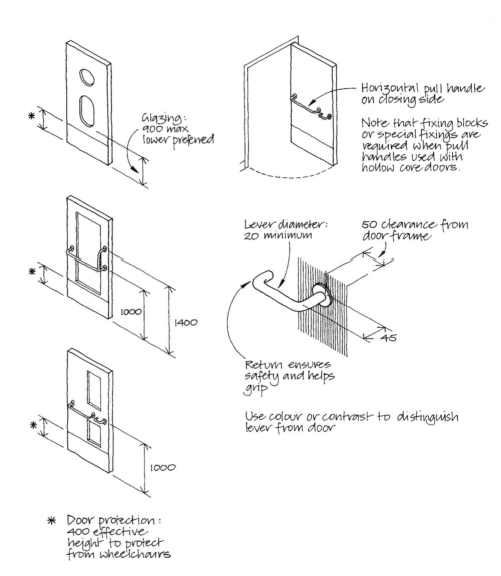

Glazing:
900 max
lower preferred

Horizontal pull handle
on closing side

Note that fixing blocks
or special fixings are
required when pull
handles used with
hollow core doors.

1000

1400

Lever diameter:
20 minimum

50 clearance from
door frame

45

Return ensures
safety and helps
grip

Use colour or contrast to distinguish
lever from door

1000

∗ Door protection:
400 effective
height to protect
from wheelchairs

FIG 25

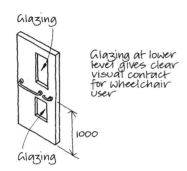

Glazing

Glazing at lower level gives clear visual contact for wheelchair user

Glazing

1000

This end of the handle will be used to pull door shut from a wheelchair

Horizontal pull handle on closing side

Note that fixing blocks or special fixings are required when pull handles are used with hollow core doors

Lever handle

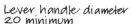

Lever handle diameter 20 minimum

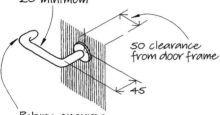

50 clearance from door frame

45

Return ensures safety and helps grip

Use colour or contrast to distinguish lever from door

Appropriate for use in church halls or other contemporary buildings

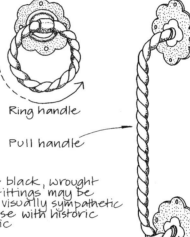

Ring handle

Pull handle

These black, wrought iron fittings may be more visually sympathetic for use with historic fabric

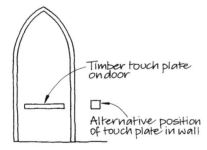

Timber touch plate on door

Alternative position of touch plate in wall

Powered door operated by touch plate (not infra red)

For manually operated doors use "push/pull" signage if possible

Lavatory doors

If door opens inwards, the door and frame must be detailed to open outwards in an emergency. This can be achieved by using double action hinges and removable stops.

If door opens outwards, a coin release indicator bolt should be fitted to provide for emergency access.

See also "Lavatories" section

FIG 26

F

G   Lavatories, together with showers and changing facilities

4.13 Provision of clearly sign-posted unisex wheelchair accessible WC facilities, designed in accordance with BS5810:1979 and Approved Document M of the Building Regulations will enable a disabled person to have assistance from a helper of different gender, and to wash their hands before transferring back to their wheelchair. Such compartments can also double up as nappy-changing points. A 'peninsular' layout permits transfer from either side of the pan and full assistance by a carer, but requires significantly more space. Travel distance should be as important a consideration as proportion of population in determining numbers and location of accessible WC compartments.

4.14 To achieve these objectives:

- the details of the design guidance of the layouts should be followed **scrupulously**;

- where more than one unisex WC compartment is provided the opportunity should be taken to hand layouts;

- the colour, or tone, of the background fittings, and any aids such as grab rails, should be contrasted to for people with visual disabilities;

- ceramic tiling and shiny floors should avoid reflections and glare which will confuse people with visual disabilities;

- slip-resistant flooring, contrasting in colour from wall surfaces, will be important for maintaining safety and hygiene;

- at least one WC compartment designed for ambulant disabled people should be provided within each range of lavatories included on any storey not accessible to wheelchair users;

- it should be ensured that suppliers and sub-contractors (eg sanitary disposal and towel suppliers) do not compromise user requirements within wheelchair WC compartments;

- management procedures should maintain the viability of the facilities;

- a method should be established through the location of equipment and training of staff for responding to any call for assistance from the user of a wheelchair WC compartment;

- the door of any WC compartment, whether used by ambulant or wheelchair users, should have the capacity to be opened outwards to ensure that entry can be gained even in the event of someone falling and blocking the doorway; and

Layout principles: wheelchair users

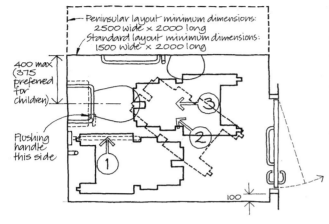

Peninsular layout minimum dimensions: 2500 wide × 2000 long

Standard layout minimum dimensions: 1500 wide × 2000 long

400 max (375 prefered for children)

Flushing handle this side

100

Layout principles: ambulant disabled

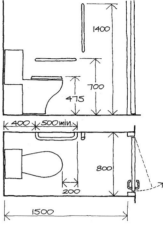

1400

700

475

400   500 min

800

200

1500

Inward opening doors may restrict access

Transfer Options

① Side transfer to wc, with wheelchair backed or driven up to rear wall

② Angled transfer using rails and/or grasping wc

③ Head on transfer using rails to pivot from wheelchair to wc

Standard layout:
This allows for use of basin and fittings from seated position on wc.
Handed layouts recommended where more than one accessible lavatory is available in a building

Peninsular layout:
This allows for approach and transfer from either side, but does not allow use of basin from wc.

Door:
Outward opening door handed to suit wheelchair approach; 100 nominal space at side helpful if door handed as shown. Although door conventionally opens outwards, it may also with advantage open inwards provided that:-
a) there is a clear minimum space of 700 × 1100 between door swing and fittings
b) the door and frame are detailed to open outwards in an emergency.

In both standard layout and peninsular layout, the space beside wc must be kept clear.

In the peninsular layout, the basin is positioned away from wheelchair manoeuvring space.

G

FIG 27

Standard Layout
1500W x 2000L minimum

The dimensions relating wc fitting to basin, associated fittings and equipment, and also to wheelchair manoeuvring space are critical for independent use. Overall dimensions shown are minimum and could, with advantage, be increased.

Peninsular Layout
2500W x 2000L minimum

Basin should be approachable in a wheelchair with all associated fittings within reach. Dispensers attached to drop down rails facilitate independent use from a seated position on the wc.

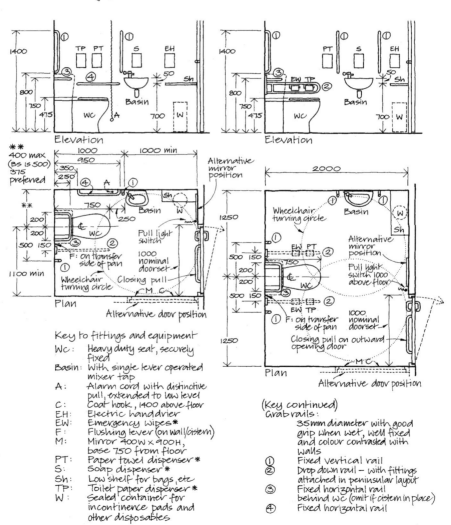

Key to fittings and equipment

Wc : Heavy duty seat, securely fixed
Basin: With single lever operated mixer tap
A: Alarm cord with distinctive pull, extended to low level
C: Coat hook, 1400 above floor
EH: Electric handdrier
EW: Emergency wipes*
F: Flushing lever (on wall/cistern)
M: Mirror 400W x 900H, base 750 from floor
PT: Paper towel dispenser *
S: Soap dispenser *
Sh: Low shelf for bags, etc
TP: Toilet paper dispenser *
W : Sealed container for incontinence pads and other disposables

(Key continued)
Grab rails:
35mm diameter with good grip when wet, well fixed and colour contrasted with walls
① Fixed vertical rail
② Drop down rail – with fittings attached in peninsular layout
③ Fixed horizontal rail behind wc (omit if cistern in place)
④ Fixed horizontal rail

FIG 28

To create the wheelchair compartment,
one wc pan, a partition and door have been removed;
a partition panel (or an existing door fixed shut) and a
new wider door have been added.

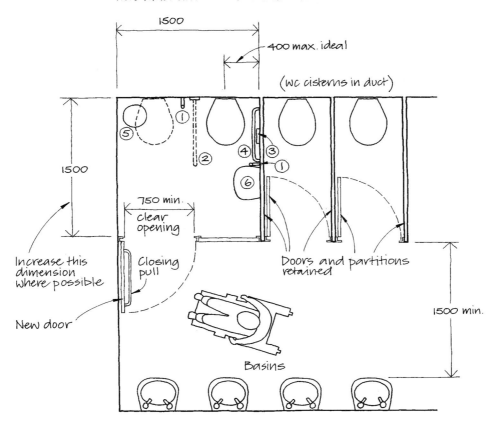

1500

400 max. ideal

(wc cisterns in duct)

1500

750 min.

clear
opening

Increase this
dimension
where possible

Closing
pull

Doors and partitions
retained

1500 min.

New door

Basins

Minimum adaptation requirements to existing
wc compartments for wheelchair access

Key

① Fixed vertical support rail
② Drop down support rail
③ Toilet paper dispenser (for single handed use)
④ Fixed horizontal support rail
⑤ Sealed container for sanitary disposables
⑥ Where practicable, a lavatory basin should
   be provided within reach of the wc from
   a seated position

FIG 29

G

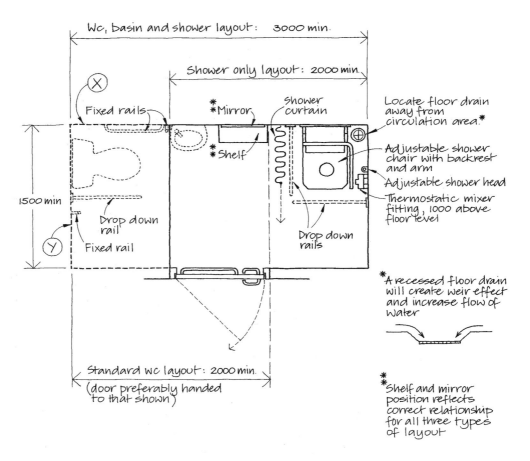

Wc pan may be on wall $\times$
with basin on side wall Y
giving a reduced overall dimension of 2600

Wc, basin and shower layout: 3000 min.

Shower only layout: 2000 min.

$\times$

Fixed rails

* Mirror

shower
curtain

Locate floor drain
away from
circulation area*

Adjustable shower
chair with backrest
and arm

Adjustable shower head

Thermostatic mixer
fitting, 1000 above
floor level

* Shelf

1500 min

Drop down
rail

Y

Fixed rail

Drop down
rails

*A recessed floor drain
will create weir effect
and increase flow of
water

Standard wc layout: 2000 min.
(door preferably handed
to that shown)

**Shelf and mirror
position reflects
correct relationship
for all three types
of layout

FIG 30

70

- any shower should be level, with no lip or rim, incorporate a seat at transfer level, a handset shower with lever operation, and thermostatic control with water temperature outlet not exceeding 43°C.

Sources

- *Building Regulations 1992, Part M Approved Document*

- *Designing for Accessibility (CAE)*

- *Buildings for All to Use (CIRIA)*

- *BS CP 5810:1979*

G

H Fixtures, fittings and equipment

4.15 In such areas as shops, meeting rooms, places of assembly, libraries, staff rooms, cafeterias, restaurants and waiting areas the installation of fittings, fixtures and equipment, as well as the layout of loose furniture should take into account possible use by people with disabilities. Shelving, where possible should be reachable from standing or seated height and counters and tables should allow knee-room for wheelchair users. Any counter or servery should have a lowered section for use from a seated position. On long circulation routes seating should be provided at intervals with space for a wheelchair alongside. Layouts of tables and chairs should allow for wheelchair manoeuvre space.

4.16 To achieve these objectives:

- fixed seating should be at a height of 475-500mm, preferably with arms for additional support and help with standing;

- all seating, whether fixed of loose, should be stable;

- any counter should have knee-space for wheelchair users and at least part of the surface at a height of 750-800mm. There should also be sufficient manoeuvre space for approach and turning away;

- lighting at glazed counters should not cause reflections that reduce the scope for lip reading;

- at fixed information points such as ticket/ enquiry offices, bank counters and post offices an induction loop system can provide hearing-aid assistance;

- when laying out seating for meetings, services for congregations, or for events attended by parents and visitors, review sight-lines, lighting, hearing aid assistance (perhaps with the provision of a temporary induction loop system), and wheelchair manoeuvre space;

- blinds, or blackout, should ensure that projected images can be clearly seen by people with impaired vision; and

- blinds, or other solar controls, should be used to ensure that low sunlight (particularly in winter) does not impair visual conditions for those with sensory disabilities or who may be seated in wheelchairs.

Sources

- *Designing for Accessibility (CAE)*

- *Buildings for All to Use (CIRIA)*

1800

1400

(A)

(C)

(B)

H

(A) Maximum shelf height to give comfortable reach for ambulant disabled person

(B) Maximum shelf height to give comfortable reach for wheelchair user

(C) Minimum height of lowest shelf : 150, preferably 300

FIG 31

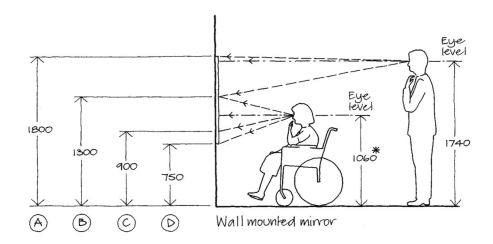

Wall mounted mirror

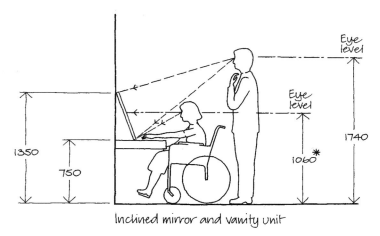

Inclined mirror and vanity unit

(A) Mirror head minimum height for ambulant user

(B) Mirror base maximum height for ambulant user

(C) Mirror base maximum height for wheelchair user

(D) Mirror base preferred height for wheelchair user

* 1060 is eye level for a seated small woman or child.
  A seated male would have an eye level of 1250

FIG 32

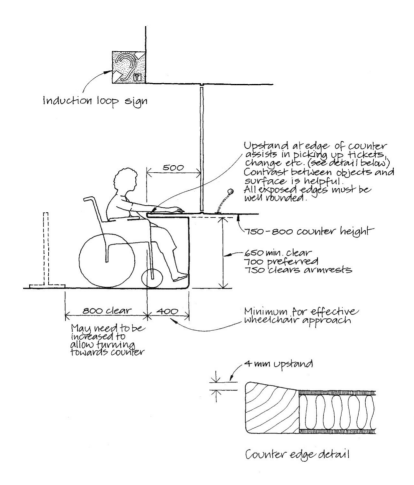

Induction loop sign

Upstand at edge of counter assists in picking up tickets, change etc. (see detail below) Contrast between objects and surface is helpful. All exposed edges must be well rounded.

500

750-800 counter height

650 min. clear
700 preferred
750 clears armrests

800 clear   400

May need to be increased to allow turning towards counter

Minimum for effective wheelchair approach

4 mm upstand

Counter edge detail

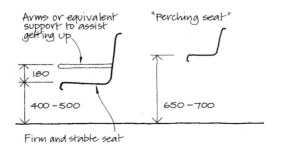

Arms or equivalent support to assist getting up

"Perching seat"

180

400-500

650-700

Firm and stable seat

FIG 33

H

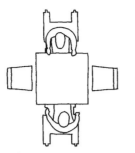

Table size 900×900

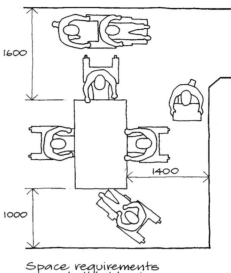

Space requirements
around all table sizes

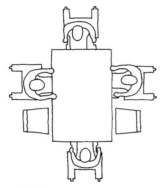

Table size 1650×1050

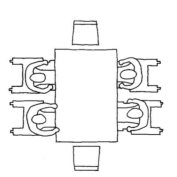

Table size 1650×1050

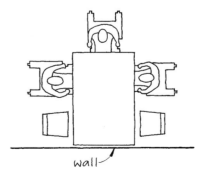

wall

Table size 1650×1050

H

FIG 34

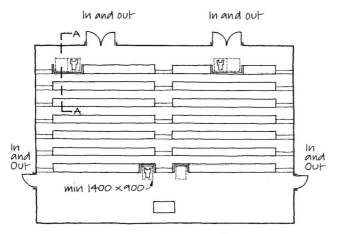

In and out   In and out

A

A

In and Out

In and Out

min 1400 × 900

Plan of a lecture theatre
Useful locations for wheelchair spaces
Each space to be minimum 1400 deep × 900 wide

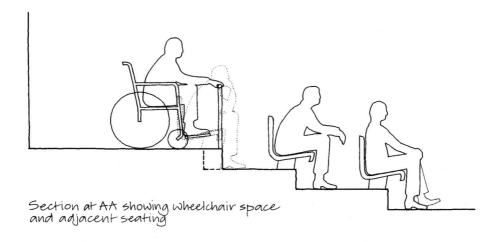

Section at AA showing wheelchair space
and adjacent seating

FIG 35

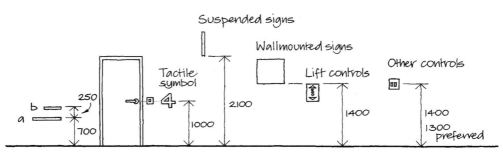

Suspended signs

Wallmounted signs

Other controls

Tactile symbol

Lift controls

250

2100

1400

1400

1300 preferred

b

a

700

1000

Reception desk
a: for wheelchair users
b: for those standing

Critical heights for signs, symbols and other circulation fittings

Hearing aid assistance

Reception
Staff assistance

Upper and lower case signage

FIG 36

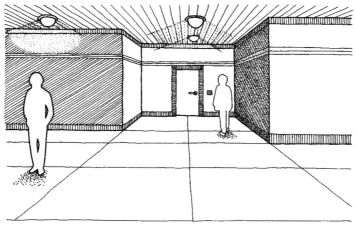

Contrast is important to help distinguish
<u>between</u> different planes

H

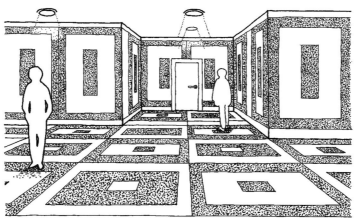

Contrast is confusing if used <u>within</u> each plane,
especially the floor plane

FIG 37

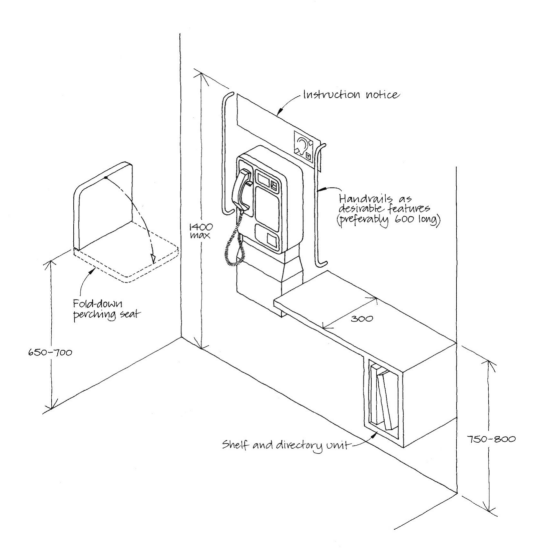

Instruction notice

Handrails as
desirable features
(preferably 600 long)

1400
max

Fold-down
perching seat

650-700

300

Shelf and directory unit

750-800

H

FIG 38

J Information and controls, including lighting, heating, communications, safety and security

4.17 The adequate provision of information, communication facilities and the scope for the independent operation of controls are all fundamental to enabling people with disabilities to use buildings without having to be assisted by others. The identification of the needs of people with sensory disabilities in the DDA means that greatly increased significance must attach to the installation of signs and information, telephones and other communication devices, hearing-aid assistance, security systems, lighting and controls. Good lighting is essential for people with visual disabilities but is equally important for those with hearing disabilities who need to be able to lip read and use sign language. The legibility and effectiveness of signage will depend on consistency, word-shape recognition through the use of upper and lower case, and contrast against background. Security systems can present particular problems for people with visual disabilities with small key pads and obscured displays. Heights of controls and the ease with which they can be read and operated will make the difference between dependence and independence. The selection of surfaces will also be very important to people with disabilities; they can make the difference between a building that is easy and comfortable to use or one that is confusing, hazardous and off-putting.

4.18 To achieve these objectives:

Lighting
- lighting should be adjustable to meeting the needs of the individual and the task on which they are working;

- lighting can be used to enhance the impact of variation in colour and texture, consequently providing visual cues which will assist people with visual disabilities or who may lack comprehension;

- uplighting, set above standing eye level, can be especially helpful in providing a glare-free environment; and

- fluorescent lighting creates a magnetic field which can cause a hum in hearing aids and should be positioned to avoid interference.

Services, including heating
- heating units should be recessed and exposed ends and angles avoided, where possible;

- fan-assisted heating systems should not add to background noise levels; and

- the main power supply cable to a building generates a considerable magnetic field that generates a loud hum in hearing aids. Its position should be clearly located and communal activities avoided in its vicinity.

J

Controls

- tone and colour contrast should be used to ensure that controls, including door furniture, are clearly distinguished from their background; and

- controls conveying information, as for lifts, should have adjacent raised letters and Braille embossing.

Hearing-aid assistance

- induction loop systems convert sound via a microphone into a magnetic field within the circuit of the loop cable. An individual within the field will be able to receive the sound, amplified by their hearing aid, and with background noise eliminated;

- induction loop systems are particularly suitable where information is given, and communication takes place from a fixed point, such as at reception, information/ booking offices in lecture rooms and assembly halls and in churches;

- sound can 'spill' out of the field and there can be overlap where loop systems are located near each other. This may make a loop system inappropriate where confidentiality is required - an infrared system can avoid this problem; and

- infrared systems convert sound into light and back again requiring a microphone, a transmitter and receiver headsets. The system can be especially useful where translation is required, it is portable and can be hired for specific events.

Telephones

- payphones are of particular importance to people with disabilities, for instance for someone with impaired mobility to call for a taxi, and should be available near to reception;

- any payphone should have an inductive coupler for use with a hearing aid; and

- telephones, and their instructions, should be fixed at a height enabling them to be used, with any display visible, from a standing or seated position; an adjacent shelf on which to be able to write is especially helpful.

Signs

- signs should use upper and lower case lettering, with letters contrasted against their background by tone and/ or colour;

- signs within reach which have embossed letters/ symbols/ Braille can be helpful to people with visual disabilities; and

- signs reassure as well as inform, and gaps in signage should be avoided on long routes.

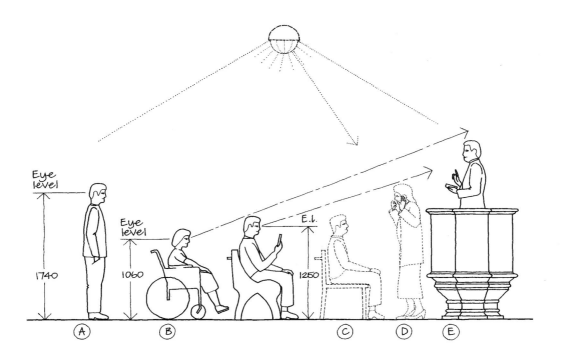

Eye level

1740

Eye level

1060

E.l.

1250

(A) (B) (C) (D) (E)

(A) Standing male

(B) Seated small woman or child.
In this position a wheelchair user's view
of altar, pulpit or lectern is likely to be obstructed

(C) Seated male

(D) A person seated in this position is likely to be
uncomfortably close to pulpit

(E) Sign language interpreter.
Face and hands must be clearly illuminated
for good lip-reading and sign interpretation
See also section "Horizontal movement and assembly"

FIG 39

J

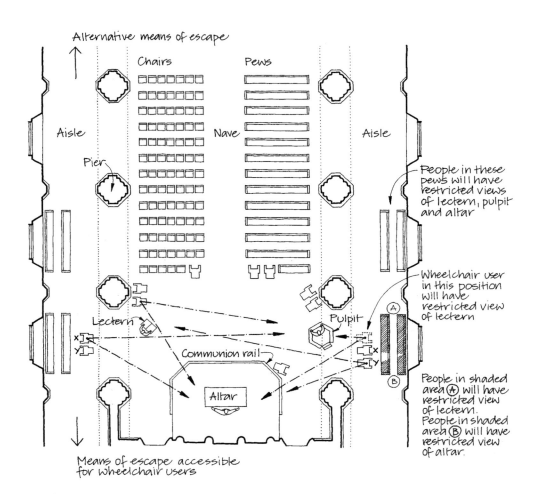

Alternative means of escape

Chairs   Pews

Aisle   Nave   Aisle

Pier

People in these pews will have restricted views of lectern, pulpit and altar

Wheelchair user in this position will have restricted view of lectern

Lectern

Pulpit

x
Y

Communion rail

Altar

Ⓐ

x
Y

Ⓑ

People in shaded area Ⓐ will have restricted view of lectern. People in shaded area Ⓑ will have restricted view of altar.

Means of escape accessible for wheelchair users

The reserved positions shown for wheelchair users give good views of altar, pulpit and lectern.

Note that hearing impaired persons in reserved positions X and Y, and in adjacent pews, may be at too acute an angle to read hand signing if sign language interpreter is near communion rail and facing towards main congregation.

FIG 40

Surfaces

- hard wall and floor surfaces increase sound reverberation and echo and can cause acoustic confusion;

- glossy wall and floor surfaces give rise to reflections and possible glare which can cause visual confusion;

- for ease of wheelchair use, floor surfaces should be firm or hard, well fixed, and non-directional. Junctions between surfaces should not create a tripping hazard and should avoid visual confusion, for instance by appearing to suggest a step or change of level where none exists;

- tone and colour contrast should be used to inform;

- textured surfaces help to inform people with visual disabilities. Texture contrast in floors can provide informative cues as can the difference between resilience and firmness;

- floor surfaces should be slip-resistant, even when wet; this is vital for ambulant disabled people and to avoid loss of confidence by older people when moving with some difficulty; and

- brightly contrasted and bold patterns to floor and wall coverings and curtains will cause confusion for people with visual disabilities. They will also make difficulties for people with hearing disabilities who have to lip read or read sign language against such a background.

Alarm and security installations

- audible alarms can, with benefit, be supplemented by visual alarms where hearing impaired people are likely to be present;

- individual alarm activated vibratory devices can be useful in specific instances; and

- entryphone systems should have an LED display for people with hearing disabilities. Digital pad and 'swipe card' operated systems should be located where they can be operated from seated or standing height.

Sources

- *Designing for Accessibility (CAE)*

- *Buildings for All to Use (CIRIA)*

- *Building Sight (RNIB)*

- *Technical Department, Induction loop systems guidance (RNID)*

J

K Means of escape

4.19 Many buildings are places of assembly and, as such, require certification by the Fire Officer. Also, unlike Part M of the Building Regulations which applies only to 'new-build', or substantially separate extensions to buildings, Part B, 'Fire Safety', applies to all buildings whether 'new-build', extended, altered or refurbished, when construction takes place. Regulation B1, 'Means of Escape', makes specific reference to BS5588 'Fire precautions in the design and construction of buildings: Part 8: Code of practice for means of escape for disabled people'. The Code is also particularly significant in providing guidance on the effective management of evacuation when construction has been completed. The Code is being substantially revised and expanded, with particular reference to management procedures and bringing it into line with 'The Fire Precautions (Places of Work) Regulations, 1997'; it is therefore especially relevant to the implementation of the DDA (see Section 5).

4.20 As well as introducing guidance for building owners and managers on means of escape, BS5588:Part 8 adopted a radical approach in acknowledging that some people, particularly those with disabilities, may require assistance to evacuate a building in an emergency. It therefore introduced the concepts of progressive horizontal evacuation on the same level, the refuge, vertical evacuation and the evacuation lift. In designing the provision for means of escape the requirements of Part B of the Building Regulations will be met if the Code is followed.

4.21 To achieve that objective:

- an 'evacuation strategy' should be put in place, with responsibility designated to individual members of staff for the assisted evacuation of people with disabilities, and they should be given appropriate training;

- that strategy should be regularly reviewed and checked for its effectiveness;

- it should include the routine checking of evacuation routes to ensure that they are kept unobstructed, free of combustible materials, and that while appropriate doors are kept locked, others can be opened in spite of security requirements;

- it should include routine checking of detectors and warning devices;

- in parts of the building which may be used by people with hearing impairments the audible alarm system should be supplemented by visual means of warning;

- individual vibratory devices, activated by operation of the central alarm system, may be appropriate in some cases;

K

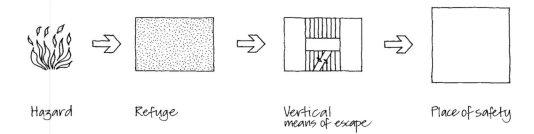

Hazard   Refuge   Vertical   Place of safety
                                 means of escape

Principles of evacuation

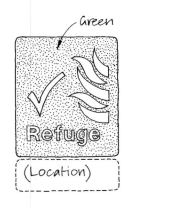

Refuge sign and location

Location reference example:
    Refuge 5
    Stairwell 3
    Floor 2

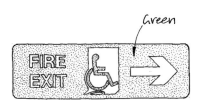

Exit symbol

FIG 41

Refuges in buildings without evacuation lifts

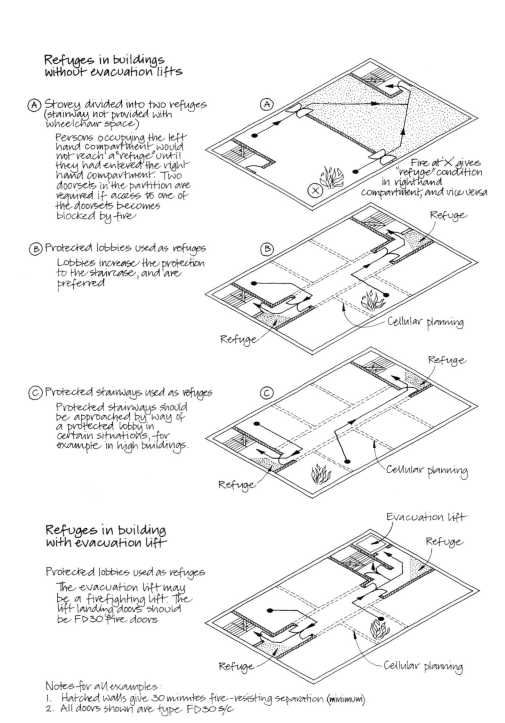

(A) Storey divided into two refuges (stairway not provided with wheelchair space)

Persons occupying the left hand compartment would not reach a "refuge" until they had entered the right hand compartment. Two doorsets in the partition are required if access to one of the doorsets becomes blocked by fire

(B) Protected lobbies used as refuges

Lobbies increase the protection to the staircase, and are preferred

(C) Protected stairways used as refuges

Protected stairways should be approached by way of a protected lobby in certain situations, for example in high buildings.

Refuges in building with evacuation lift

Protected lobbies used as refuges

The evacuation lift may be a firefighting lift. The lift landing doors should be FD30 fire doors

Fire at 'X' gives "refuge" condition in righthand compartment, and vice versa

Refuge

Cellular planning

Refuge

Refuge

Cellular planning

Refuge

Evacuation lift

Refuge

Cellular planning

Refuge

Notes for all examples:
1. Hatched walls give 30 minutes fire-resisting separation (minimum)
2. All doors shown are type FD30 s/c

FIG 42

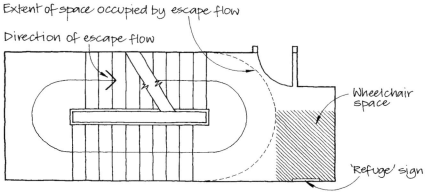

Extent of space occupied by escape flow

Direction of escape flow

Wheelchair space

'Refuge' sign

(A)   Access to the wheelchair space is in the same direction as the escape flow

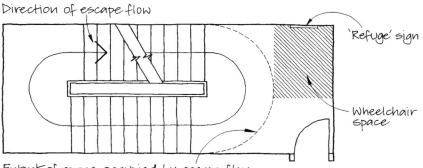

Direction of escape flow

'Refuge' sign

Wheelchair space

(B)   Extent of space occupied by escape flow

Access to the wheelchair space is against the escape flow

Wheelchair spaces in protected stairways

FIG 43

K

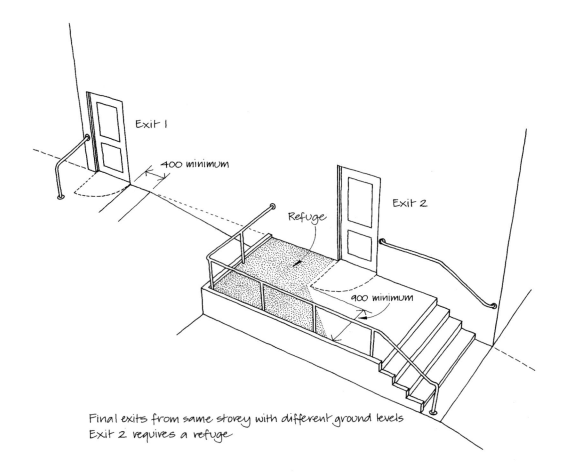

Exit 1

400 minimum

Refuge

Exit 2

900 minimum

Final exits from same storey with different ground levels
Exit 2 requires a refuge

K

FIG 44

- in multi-storey buildings the introduction of at least one 'evacuation lift' with a protected power supply should be considered;

- in multi-storey buildings refuges should be identified and appropriately sign-posted;

- where a refuge is not related to an 'evacuation lift' the provision of the means of assisted evacuation, such as a 'carry-chair' should be considered; and

- final exit routes from buildings, particularly where they are related to vertical evacuation, should be as accessible to wheelchair users as are entry routes. If steps are necessary at the exit point an external refuge should be formed from which assisted evacuation can be effected, if needs be by the Fire Brigade.

Sources

- *Building Regulations 1992, Part B Approved Document*

- *BS 5588:Part 8 Code of Practice for Means of Escape for Disabled People*

- *Designing for Accessibility (CAE)*

- *Buildings for All to Use (CIRIA)*

- *Building Sight (RNIB)*

K

5.00 ACCESSIBILITY, SAFETY AND SECURITY: RISK ASSESSMENT AND EVACUATION PLANNING - MANAGEMENT ISSUES

5.01 No one can any longer be unaware of the problems of security that arise in relation to buildings in public use, including all workplaces. In the age of the computer, theft of high-value, high-tech property is endemic, but more disturbingly settings which traditionally used to be regarded as safe, or perhaps even sacrosanct, are no longer so. Churches now are largely kept locked except when actively watched; and recent events involving wholly unexpected attacks on both children and staff have prompted all schools to introduce extensive security arrangements. Even hospitals have had to introduce security systems to protect both patients and staff. In many urban areas, particularly, there has also proved to be an increasingly frequent and damaging incidence of vandalism.

5.02 In consequence, most buildings now tend to have restricted and closely monitored access, often at a single point of entry. All exits from buildings, including fire exits, tend to be secured, with door furniture which can be released from the interior for emergency evacuation, but can only be opened externally, if at all, by key operation. Windows too, particularly at ground floor level, now tend to be security latched and restricted, and doors and windows may well be alarm linked. Many premises have also installed security lighting around their perimeter. All these measures, while regrettably necessary to protect their occupants, reduce the accessibility of buildings, giving rise to conflicts between accessibility, security and safety.

5.03 While some of the difficulties arising from these conflicts can be resolved through appropriate specification (for instance of key-coded or 'swipe' pad operated door release mechanisms, of push bar or lever operated door furniture together with the addition of door bells or 'voice-to-voice' units to signal for help) many problems can be overcome by modified management procedures and staff training.

5.10 Procedures in case of fire

5.11 Evacuation procedures should be pre-planned by those having control of buildings together with the fire authority. It is essential to identify the needs of disabled people and to make arrangements for their assistance. Staff training and knowledge of how to implement procedures is a vital part of any effective evacuation programme and should be confirmed in writing. The procedures should be tested at least once a year, and any amendments also confirmed in writing.

5.12 In all workplaces all employees should have appropriate training in evacuation procedures. Designated staff should have responsibility for overseeing the evacuation of colleagues with disabilities. Visitors with disabilities may not be previously identified by staff, but should identify themselves in the event of an emergency.

5.13 In the event of an evacuation, as the result of a fire, some disabled people will temporarily remain in refuges while waiting for help to move to a final exit and safety. In that event there are three essential communication requirements:

1) Those organizing the evacuation of the building need to know:

   • how many disabled people there are;

   • the nature of their need for assistance; and

   • the refuge or refuges in which they are located.

2) The disabled people in each refuge need to be reassured that their presence there is known to the building management; and

3) In order to meet these requirements it is desirable that there is a system of two-way communication, usable by disabled people, between those waiting in a refuge and those organizing the evacuation.

4) It will also be important that evacuation organizers understand the techniques for assisting disabled people. For instance, those with visual disabilities will need their sighted helper to walk just ahead of them, and having taken their helper's arm, allow them to take movement cues from them; or how a wheelchair user should be carried, preferably in their own wheelchair, or alternatively in a 'carry-chair'. (Guidance can be sought from the organisations listed in Appendix A.)

5) Guidance on the use of 'Evacuation Lifts', and the procedures for staff in their operation is to be found in BS 5588:Part 8, referred to in Appendix A, as can examples of fire-plan strategies in buildings provided with 'Evacuation Lifts'.

6) In buildings without 'Evacuation Lifts' the recommended sequence for evacuation is as follows:

- on hearing the alarm, disabled people should move to the nearest refuge;

- the designated, trained and competent person, after completing their evacuation/ search procedure, moves to the refuge; and

- disabled persons at the refuge(s) are assisted down (up) the stairway towards the final exit level.

5.20 Fire alarm systems

5.21 In the event of a fire it is essential that all the occupants of the building are alerted as speedily as possible. Any fire alarm system installed for the majority of building users and complying with BS 5839:Part 1 should also be suitable for disabled people. This might mean, for instance, that audible alarm signals might need to be supplemented by visual signals. These should be the subject of consultation with the fire authority, as, generally, hearing disabled people will either be able to perceive an audible alarm signal, or they may reliably be alerted by other occupants. It is not safe to rely on hearing impaired people being alerted by visual warning systems, as in certain conditions such as bright sunlight, the effectiveness of such systems is overwhelmed.

5.22 The recommendations given in BS 5839:Part 1 for the number and siting of manual call points should be adequate for the speedy initiation of the fire alarm in most buildings. Consideration should also be given, however, to the following if the alarm is likely to need to be initiated by a disabled person:

- the provision of an automatic fire detection system;

- a reduction in the spacing between manual call points to compensate for delays in operation because of the limited mobility of the occupants; and

- the provision of alternative manually operated switching devices (eg ceiling cord switches, etc) additional to those recommended in BS 5839:Part 1, where operation of the manual call points is likely to be difficult or seriously delayed because of the occupants' disabilities.

5.23 In certain situations, such as a generally noisy area where audible alarms may not be heard by a hearing impaired person, especially one who might be working on their own, alternative types of alarm signal may be necessary, such as visual alarms, paging systems, vibrating devices or sound signals within carefully selected frequency bands.

The type of alarm chosen should be appropriate in relation to the activities being carried out in the areas being considered. Technical guidance on the selection of suitable devices may be obtained from the RNID, 19-23 Featherstone Street, London EC1Y 8SL. (Technical aids/ adaptations supplier, RNID/ Sound Advantage, 1 Metro Centre, Welbeck Way, Peterborough PE2 7UH.)

5.30 Building management

5.31 Accessibility can not be achieved only by good design. The way that a building is managed and operated, day-by-day, will also do much to determine how accessible it is for disabled people. All too frequently clear passage through a corridor is compromised by 'temporary' storage of boxes; the addition of 'ad-hoc' signs compromise an effective signage system; the installation of an induction loop system is rendered ineffective because its presence is not publicised. The issue of accessibility should be touched upon in all parts of any 'Building Management Manual', as well as being identified as a section in its own right. The reasoning behind requirements should be explained.

5.32 The kind of information given might be as follows:

- *Car parking*
  – ensure that non-disabled drivers do not occupy spaces provided for disabled people;

- *Routes*
  – ensure that external routes, ramps and steps are kept clean and unobstructed, free of leaves and of ice and snow in winter;

- *Doors*
  – ensure that door closers are regularly maintained, pressure is kept to the minimum necessary, and that door furniture is clean and free-moving;

- *Horizontal movement*
  – ensure that spaces needed for wheelchair manoeuvre, or used by people with impaired vision, are not obstructed by deliveries or storage;

- *Vertical movement*
  – ensure that any lift car levels accurately and that short rise lifts are not abused;

- *Lavatories*
  – ensure that supplies of toilet paper and paper towels are regularly replenished without WC spaces being used for 'unofficial' storage;

  – also ensure that suppliers and contractors, such as sanitary disposal do not compromise transfer space by placement of their bins;

- *Signs*
  - ensure that 'ad-hoc' signs are replaced by signs integrated into the signage system, and that they are correctly re-fixed after redecoration;

- *Induction loop systems*
  - ensure that installations are publicised and their functioning checked regularly;

- *Alarms and security*
  - ensure that alarm systems, including any assistance call provisions from WCs, are checked regularly, and that new staff are trained in alarm response procedures, including a clear understanding of instructions for, and constraints upon, lifting and handling;

- *Surfaces*
  - ensure that cleaning and polishing procedures do not render slip-resistant surfaces ineffective;

  - also ensure that flooring material junctions do not become worn or mats loosened to form a tripping hazard;

  - also ensure that when redecoration takes place it does not compromise valuable existing provision of cues, contrast, tone and texture;

  - where redecoration takes place colour/ contrast is reinstated; if necessary, in relationship to such items as door frames, control panels, signs, etc;

- *Lighting*
  - ensure that windows, lamps and blinds are kept clean in order to avoid loss of light and deterioration in light quality;

  - also ensure that blown lamps and tubes which have failed or are starting to flicker are replaced immediately.

5.33 There will, of course, be many further sections, relating specifically to the particular building and its functions. As accessibility issues emerge they should give rise to the addition of new sections to the Manual, with guidance provided on problem resolution and prevention.

APPENDIX A
INFORMATION SOURCES AND REFERENCES

6.00 APPENDIX A
INFORMATION SOURCES AND REFERENCES

6.01 Centre for Accessible Environments
Nutmeg House, 60 Gainsford Street, London SE1 2NY
Tel: 0171 357 8183 Fax: 0171 357 8183

References:

'Designing for Accessibility - an introductory guide' Tessa Palfreyman, 1993.

'Specifiers' Handbook 1, Electrical Controls' Tessa Palfreyman, 1990.

'Specifiers' Handbook 2, Wheelchair Stairlifts and Platform Lifts' Stephen Thorpe, 1993.

'Good Loo Design Guide' Stephen Thorpe, 1988.

'Wheelchair Template' Stephen Thorpe, 1991.

The Centre offers information services and training in relationship to disability and built environments, and offers an extensive range of publications.

6.02 CIRIA, Construction Industry Research and Information Association
6 Storey's Gate, London SW1P 3AU
Tel: 0171 222 8891 Fax: 0171 222 1708

Reference:

'Buildings for All to Use: good practice guidance for improving existing public buildings for people with disabilities' Sylvester Bone, 1996.

Comprehensive guidance prepared in anticipation of the DDA.

6.03 DOE, Department of Environment, Transport and Regions

Reference:

'The Building Regulations 1991' (1999 Edition).
Approved Document M, 'Access and facilities for disabled people'.
Approved Document B, 'Fire safety'.

HMSO, HMSO Publications Centre, PO Box 276 London SW8 5DT
Tel (Orders): 0171 873 0011   Fax (Orders): 0171 873 8200
Tel (General Enquiries): 0171 873 0011

6.04 English Heritage
23 Savile Row, London W1X 1AB
Tel: 0171 973 3434

Reference:

'Easy Access to Historic Properties' 1995.

Statement of policy, and setting out of guidance in relationship to achieving access to historic buildings. Essential reference when adapting and altering 'Listed Buildings'.

Also:
'Access to the Historic Environment' Lisa Foster (Consultant to English Heritage), 1997.

6.05 BSI (British Standard Codes of Practice)
2 Park Street, London W1A 2BS
Tel: 0171 629 9000

References:

BS5810:1979 Code of Practice for Access for the Disabled to Buildings.
BS5588 Part 8:1988 Fire Precautions in the Design, Construction and Use of Buildings -
Code of Practice for Means of Escape for Disabled People.

6.06 RNIB, Royal National Institute for the Blind
224 Great Portland Street, London W1N 6AA
Tel: 0171 388 1266 Fax: 0171 388 2034

Reference:

'Building Sight' Peter Barker, *et al.* 1995.

Comprehensive design guidance for people with visual disabilities.

6.07 **RNID**, Royal National Institute for Deaf People
19-23 Featherstone Street, London EC1Y 8SL
Tel: 0171 296 8000 Fax: 0171 296 8199

References:

'Louder than Words' Alec Miskin, 1995.

'Induction Loops in Public Places' [Leaflet].

Design and technical guidance, and technical advisory and installation service.

6.08 **DfEE**, Department for Education and Employment
Architects & Buildings Branch, Sanctuary Buildings, Great Smith Street,
London SW1P 3BT
Tel: 0171 925 5971 Fax: 0171 925 6986

DfEE Publications
PO Box 5050, Sudbury, Suffolk CO10 6ZQ
Tel: 0845 60 222 60 Fax: 0845 60 333 60
Email: dfee@prologcs.demon.co.uk

References:

'What the Disability Discrimination Act (DDA) 1995 Means for
Schools and LEAs' [Circular number 3/97].

Available free of charge from:
DfEE Publications Centre, PO Box 6927, London E3 3NZ
Tel: 0171 510 0150 Fax: 0171 510 0196

'Designing for Children with Special Educational Needs, Ordinary Schools'
[Building Bulletin 61].

'Excellence for all Children: Meeting Special Educational Needs'
[Green Paper: October 1997].

'Access for Disabled People to School Buildings: Management and Design Guide'
[Building Bulletin 91 (Spring 1999)].

Available form the Stationery Office (see below).

6.09 Department of Health

'A Practical Guide for Disabled People - Where to Find Information, Services and Equipment'.

Available from the Stationery Office (see below).

Also available in Braille and audio-cassette from
Department of Health
PO Box 410, Wetherby LS23 7LN

6.10 HM Government

'Disability Discrimination Act 1995'.

The Stationery Office
PO Box 276, London SW8 5DT
Tel (Orders): 0171 873 9090 Fax (Orders): 0171 873 8200
Tel (General Enquiries): 0171 873 8200

6.11 Council for the Care of Churches

'Widening the Eye of the Needle: Access to Church Buildings for People with Disabilities'
John Penton.

Church House Publishing
Church House, Great Smith Street, London SW1P 3NZ

Guidance on alterations to churches, including reference to ecclesiastical procedures, and work to sensitive historic fabric.

6.12 Further advice and reference can be obtained by contacting:

John H Penton, Consultant Architect & Designer
8 Spicer Street, St Albans, Hertfordshire AL3 4PQ
Tel: 01727 868 873 Fax: 01727 852 376

APPENDIX B
ACCESSIBILITY AUDIT REPORTS

7.00 APPENDIX B
ACCESS AUDIT CHECKLIST

Ref	Title	Sheet No.
A	Approach and car parking	01
B	Routes and external level change, including ramps and steps	02
C	Entrances, including reception	03/ 04
D	Horizontal movement and activities	05/ 06
E	Vertical movement and internal level change	07/ 08
F	Doors	09
G	Lavatories	10/ 11
H	Fixtures, fittings and equipment	12
J	Information and controls	13
K	Means of escape	14
S	Supplementary (referenced S/01 to 20)	S/-
AN	Attached note	AN/-

Checklist sheets should be completed with relevance to all the specific areas to which they apply. Additional information should be firmly attached using the 'Attached notes' and clearly cross referenced. 'Supplementary sheets' should be attached as necessary. More than one checklist sheet should be used for differing areas when appropriate, eg when a number of individual buildings or departments may be involved.

Boxes should be completed, or left blank, in relation to those areas surveyed, and deletions made where choices can be eliminated. A blank should be seen as a positive means of completing the pro-forma, reflecting a situation that can be assessed as essentially neutral or satisfactory.

Copies of the Accessibility Audit Reports, Attached notes and Supplementary sheets are available from RIBA Publications.

Accessibility Audit Report
Access Audit Checklist

Date _____

Location _____

	Wheelchair	Ambulant	Dexterity	Visual	Auditory	Comprehension	
✗ applicable	✗	✗	✗	✗	✗	✗	note

1 Is the building within convenient walking distance of:

(a) a public highway?	☐	☐	☐	☐	☐	☐	_____
(b) public transport?	☐	☐	☐	☐	☐	☐	_____
(c) car parking?	☐	☐	☐	☐	☐	☐	_____
2 ☐ Is the route clearly marked/ found?	☐	☐	☐	☐	☐	☐	_____
3 ☐ Is the route free of kerbs?	☐	☐	☐	☐	☐	☐	_____
4 ☐ Is the surface smooth and slip-resistant?	☐	☐	☐	☐	☐	☐	_____
5 ☐ Is the route wide enough?	☐	☐	☐	☐	☐	☐	_____
6 ☐ Is it free of such hazards as bollards, litter bins, outward opening windows and doors or overhanging projections?	☐	☐	☐	☐	☐	☐	_____
7 ☐ Is it adequately lit?	☐	☐	☐	☐	☐	☐	_____
8 ☐ Is it identified by visual, audible and tactile information?	☐	☐	☐	☐	☐	☐	_____
9 ☐ Is there car parking for people with reduced mobility?	☐	☐	☐	☐	☐	☐	_____
10 ☐ Is it clearly marked out, signed, easily found and kept free from misuse?	☐	☐	☐	☐	☐	☐	_____
11 ☐ Is it as near the entrance as possible?	☐	☐	☐	☐	☐	☐	_____
12 ☐ Is it suitably surfaced?	☐	☐	☐	☐	☐	☐	_____
13 ☐ Is the route to the building kept free of snow, ice and fallen leaves?	☐	☐	☐	☐	☐	☐	_____
14 ☐ Is the route level (ie no gradient steeper than 1:20 and no steps)?	☐	☐	☐	☐	☐	☐	_____

See checklist B, sheet 2

Routes and external level change, including ramps and steps

Sheet 02

Page No......

B

Accessibility Audit Report
Access Audit Checklist

Date _____

Location _____

✗ applicable

		Wheelchair ✗	Ambulant ✗	Dexterity ✗	Visual ✗	Auditory ✗	Comprehension ✗	note
1	☐ Is there a ramp, with level surfaces at <u>top/ intermediate / bottom</u>? (delete)	☐	☐	☐	☐	☐	☐	_____
2	☐ Is it wide enough and suitably graded? (max 1:12, 1:15 or less, preferred)	☐	☐	☐	☐	☐	☐	_____
3	☐ Is the surface slip-resistant?	☐	☐	☐	☐	☐	☐	_____
4	☐ Are there kerbs and are the edges protected to prevent accidents?	☐	☐	☐	☐	☐	☐	_____
5	☐ Are there handrails to <u>one</u> or <u>both</u> side(s)? (delete)	☐	☐	☐	☐	☐	☐	_____
6	☐ If a permanent ramp (or regraded levels) can not be formed (perhaps to a Listed Building), is a portable ramp available?	☐	☐	☐	☐	☐	☐	_____
7	☐ Are there (<u>alternative</u>) steps? (delete)	☐	☐	☐	☐	☐	☐	_____
8	☐ Identified by visual/ tactile information?	☐	☐	☐	☐	☐	☐	_____
9	☐ Are there handrails to <u>one</u> or <u>both</u> side(s)? (delete)	☐	☐	☐	☐	☐	☐	_____
10	☐ Are ramps and steps adequately lit?	☐	☐	☐	☐	☐	☐	_____
11	☐ Are treads and risers consistent in depth and height?	☐	☐	☐	☐	☐	☐	_____
12	☐ Are all nosings <u>marked</u> and/ or <u>readily identifiable</u>? (delete)	☐	☐	☐	☐	☐	☐	_____
13	☐ Are landings of <u>adequate size</u> and are they provided at <u>intermediate levels</u> in long flights? (delete)	☐	☐	☐	☐	☐	☐	_____
14	☐ If safe and convenient ramps and steps can not be provided is vertical movement by powered means an alternative? **See checklist E, sheets 7, 8 and 9**	☐	☐	☐	☐	☐	☐	_____

Accessibility Audit Report
Access Audit Checklist

Date _____

Location _____

C

		Wheelchair	Ambulant	Dexterity	Visual	Auditory	Comprehension	note
✗ applicable		✗	✗	✗	✗	✗	✗	
1 ☐	Is the door clearly distinguishable from the façade?	☐	☐	☐	☐	☐	☐	_____
2 ☐	If glass, is it visible when closed?	☐	☐	☐	☐	☐	☐	_____
3 ☐	Does the clear door opening or one leaf when opened permit passage of a wheelchair or double buggy? (delete)	☐	☐	☐	☐	☐	☐	_____
4 ☐	Does it have a level flush threshold, and a recessed matwell? (delete)	☐	☐	☐	☐	☐	☐	_____
5 ☐	Is there visibility through the doorway from both sides at standing and seated levels? (delete)	☐	☐	☐	☐	☐	☐	_____
6 ☐	Is there a minimum 300mm wide wheelchair manoeuvre space beside the leading edge of the door to clear the doorswing?	☐	☐	☐	☐	☐	☐	_____
7 ☐	Can the door furniture be used at both standing and seated height? (delete)	☐	☐	☐	☐	☐	☐	_____
8 ☐	Can it be easily grasped and operated?	☐	☐	☐	☐	☐	☐	_____
9 ☐	If the door has a closer mechanism does it have:							
☐	(a) delayed closure action?	☐	☐	☐	☐	☐	☐	_____
☐	(b) slow-action closure?	☐	☐	☐	☐	☐	☐	_____
☐	(c) minimal closure pressure?	☐	☐	☐	☐	☐	☐	_____
10 ☐	If the door is power-operated does it have visual and tactile information?	☐	☐	☐	☐	☐	☐	_____
11 ☐	If the door is security-protected is the system suitable for use by and within reach of people with sensory or mobility impairments?	☐	☐	☐	☐	☐	☐	_____
12 ☐	If there is a lobby do the inner and outer doors meet the same criteria?	☐	☐	☐	☐	☐	☐	_____

© John Penton

continued

Accessibility Audit Report
Access Audit Checklist

Date _____

Location _____

		Wheelchair	Ambulant	Dexterity	Visual	Auditory	Comprehension	note
✗ applicable		✗	✗	✗	✗	✗	✗	
13 ☐	Does the lobby layout enable all users to clear one door before passing through the next?	☐	☐	☐	☐	☐	☐	_____
14 ☐	Are signs designed and positioned to inform those with visual impairments, and wheelchair users with reduced eye-levels?	☐	☐	☐	☐	☐	☐	_____
15 ☐	Does the lighting installation take in to account the needs of people with visual impairments?	☐	☐	☐	☐	☐	☐	_____
16 ☐	Are floor surfaces:							
☐	(a) slip-resistant, even when wet?	☐	☐	☐	☐	☐	☐	_____
☐	(b) so hard that they cause accoustic confusion?	☐	☐	☐	☐	☐	☐	_____
☐	(c) firm for wheelchair manoeuvre?	☐	☐	☐	☐	☐	☐	_____
17 ☐	Do junctions between floor surfaces present tripping hazards or cause visual confusion?	☐	☐	☐	☐	☐	☐	_____
18 ☐	Is any reception point suitable for approach and use from both sides by people in standing and seated positions?	☐	☐	☐	☐	☐	☐	_____
19 ☐	Is it fitted with an induction loop?	☐	☐	☐	☐	☐	☐	_____
20 ☐	If a public telephone is available is it, and the instructions:							
☐	(a) at a height suitable for all users?	☐	☐	☐	☐	☐	☐	_____
☐	(b) equipped with inductive coupling?	☐	☐	☐	☐	☐	☐	_____
21 ☐	For those progressing to other parts of the building is information provided by signs, supported by tactile information such as a map or a model?	☐	☐	☐	☐	☐	☐	_____

Accessibility Audit Report
Access Audit Checklist

Date _____

Location _____

D

	Wheelchair	Ambulant	Dexterity	Visual	Auditory	Comprehension	note

✗ applicable

✗ ✗ ✗ ✗ ✗ ✗

1 ☐ Is any corridor/ passageway/ aisle wide enough for a wheelchair user to manoeuvre and for other people to pass?
☐ ☐ ☐ ☐ ☐ ☐ _____

2 ☐ Is any corridor, etc, free from obstruction to wheelchair users and hazards to people with impaired vision?
☐ ☐ ☐ ☐ ☐ ☐ _____

3 ☐ Do any lobbies allow users (including wheelchair users) to clear one door before approaching the next with minimal manoeuvre?
☐ ☐ ☐ ☐ ☐ ☐ _____

4 ☐ Is turning space available for wheelchair users?
☐ ☐ ☐ ☐ ☐ ☐ _____

5 ☐ Do natural and artificial lighting avoid glare and silhouetting?
☐ ☐ ☐ ☐ ☐ ☐ _____

6 ☐ Are there visual clues for orientation?
☐ ☐ ☐ ☐ ☐ ☐ _____

7 ☐ Do floor surfaces:
☐ (a) allow ease of movement for wheelchair users?
☐ (b) avoid light reflection and sound reverberation?
☐ ☐ ☐ ☐ ☐ ☐ _____
☐ ☐ ☐ ☐ ☐ ☐ _____

8 ☐ Do textured surfaces convey useful information for people with impaired vision?
☐ ☐ ☐ ☐ ☐ ☐ _____

9 ☐ Are direction or information signs (including means of escape) visible from both sitting and standing levels, and are they in <u>upper</u> and <u>lower</u> case (delete), and in large enough type to be read by those with impaired vision?
☐ ☐ ☐ ☐ ☐ ☐ _____

10 ☐ Are there tactile signs and information for those with impaired vision?
☐ ☐ ☐ ☐ ☐ ☐ _____

11 ☐ Is the maintenance of these items checked regularly?
☐ ☐ ☐ ☐ ☐ ☐ _____

12 ☐ Is lighting designed to meet a wide range of needs?
☐ ☐ ☐ ☐ ☐ ☐ _____

© John Penton

continued

Accessibility Audit Report
Access Audit Checklist

Date _____

Location _____

D

		Wheelchair	Ambulant	Dexterity	Visual	Auditory	Comprehension	note
✗ applicable		✗	✗	✗	✗	✗	✗	
13 ☐	Is sufficient circulation space allowed for wheelchair users?	☐	☐	☐	☐	☐	☐	_____
14 ☐	Is it maintained clear of obstructions which could create hazards for people with visual disabilities?	☐	☐	☐	☐	☐	☐	_____
15 ☐	Are seating arrangements/ spaces suitable for use by people with visual disabilities?	☐	☐	☐	☐	☐	☐	_____
16 ☐	Are all areas of assembly/ meeting equipped with an induction loop system?	☐	☐	☐	☐	☐	☐	_____
17 ☐	If the use of an induction loop system is precluded is an infrared system checked regularly?	☐	☐	☐	☐	☐	☐	_____
18 ☐	Is the functioning and operation of the induction loop or infrared system checked regularly?	☐	☐	☐	☐	☐	☐	_____
19 ☐	Are telephones fitted with inductive loop couplers?	☐	☐	☐	☐	☐	☐	_____
20 ☐	Is a minicom available for use by people with hearing disabilities?	☐	☐	☐	☐	☐	☐	_____

Accessibility Audit Report
Access Audit Checklist

Date _____

Location _____

E

✗ applicable

	Wheelchair	Ambulant	Dexterity	Visual	Auditory	Comprehension	note
	✗	✗	✗	✗	✗	✗	
1 ☐ Is the location of any <u>step/ ramp</u> clearly indicated by use of <u>sign/ colour</u> contrast/ texture/ lighting? (delete)	☐	☐	☐	☐	☐	☐	_____
2 ☐ Does any <u>step/ stairs/ ramp</u> have a handrail to <u>one/ both</u> side(s), and do(es) <u>it/ they</u> extend 300mm beyond the top and bottom of any flight? (delete)	☐	☐	☐	☐	☐	☐	_____
3 ☐ Is any level change clearly lit?	☐	☐	☐	☐	☐	☐	_____
4 ☐ Is the pitch (risers and treads) of <u>steps/ stairs</u> or any <u>ramp</u> consistent, and are nosings clearly identifiable? (delete)	☐	☐	☐	☐	☐	☐	_____
5 ☐ If there are landings are they large enough to permit passing and turning manoeuvres, and are they provided in any long flight?	☐	☐	☐	☐	☐	☐	_____
6 ☐ Is any short rise within a single storey ramped; if so, is the ramped surface indicated and is it slip-resistant?	☐	☐	☐	☐	☐	☐	_____
7 ☐ Does any ramp pitch steepness exceed <u>1:12/ 1:15/ 1:20/ 1:20+</u>? (delete)	☐	☐	☐	☐	☐	☐	_____
8 ☐ If a permanent ramp can not be provided (perhaps in a Listed Building) can a moveable ramp be made available?	☐	☐	☐	☐	☐	☐	_____
9 ☐ Are steps available as an alternative to any ramp or ramped surface?	☐	☐	☐	☐	☐	☐	_____
10 ☐ Where level change is less than a full storey in height is a power-operated system appropriate? <u>(Platform Lift/ Stairlift/ Lift</u> (delete)) - **See checklists G and H, sheets 11, 12 and 13.**	☐	☐	☐	☐	☐	☐	_____
11 ☐ Platform Lift: ☐ (a) are the controls at <u>both</u> levels identifiable and reachable from <u>sitting</u> and <u>standing</u> levels? (delete)	☐	☐	☐	☐	☐	☐	_____
☐ (b) is the platform adequate for wheelchair use and manoeuvre?	☐	☐	☐	☐	☐	☐	_____
☐ (c) in the event of a power failure does the platform return to lower level?	☐	☐	☐	☐	☐	☐	_____
☐ (d) is the equipment maintained and its operation checked regularly?	☐	☐	☐	☐	☐	☐	_____

continued

Accessibility Audit Report
Access Audit Checklist

Date _____

Location _____

E

✗ applicable

	Wheelchair	Ambulant	Dexterity	Visual	Auditory	Comprehension	note
	✗	✗	✗	✗	✗	✗	

12 ☐ Stairlift:

☐ (a) are the controls at all levels identifiable and reachable from <u>sitting</u> and <u>standing</u> levels? (delete)

	☐	☐	☐	☐	☐	☐	_____

☐ (b) is the platform adequate for wheelchair use and manoeuvre?

	☐	☐	☐	☐	☐	☐	_____

☐ (c) is approach <u>convenient</u> and <u>safe</u> at all appropriate landings? (delete)

	☐	☐	☐	☐	☐	☐	_____

☐ (d) does the stairlift have a 'soft-start' action?

	☐	☐	☐	☐	☐	☐	_____

☐ (e) when not in use is the platform powered to fold away to avoid obstruction?

	☐	☐	☐	☐	☐	☐	_____

☐ (f) in the event of a power failure does the platform return to lower level?

	☐	☐	☐	☐	☐	☐	_____

☐ (g) is the equipment maintained and its operation checked regularly?

	☐	☐	☐	☐	☐	☐	_____

13 ☐ Lift:

☐ (a) is the lift's location clearly defined by <u>visual</u> and <u>tactile</u> information? (delete)

	☐	☐	☐	☐	☐	☐	_____

☐ (b) are controls at all floors visible, identifiable and reachable from <u>sitting</u> and <u>standing</u> levels? (delete)

	☐	☐	☐	☐	☐	☐	_____

☐ (c) is there adequate, unobstructed space at each floor lift entry for wheelchair manoeuvre?

	☐	☐	☐	☐	☐	☐	_____

☐ (d) does the lift door open widely enough for wheelchair user access?

	☐	☐	☐	☐	☐	☐	_____

☐ (e) does door operation allow slow entry and exit?

	☐	☐	☐	☐	☐	☐	_____

☐ (f) do the lift car internal dimensions allow sufficient space for a <u>wheelchair user</u> and <u>carer</u>? (delete)

	☐	☐	☐	☐	☐	☐	_____

☐ (g) does the car have appropriate support rails?

	☐	☐	☐	☐	☐	☐	_____

☐ (h) are the lift car controls, including emergency call, located within reach of all users and with visual and tactile information?

	☐	☐	☐	☐	☐	☐	_____

☐ (i) is there audible floor indication?

	☐	☐	☐	☐	☐	☐	_____

☐ (j) is the lift an 'Evacuation Lift'?
See checklist K, sheet 15

	☐	☐	☐	☐	☐	☐	_____

☐ (k) is the lift regularly maintained and its functional operation routinely checked?

	☐	☐	☐	☐	☐	☐	_____

© John Penton

116

Accessibility Audit Report
Access Audit Checklist

Date _____

Location _____

		Wheelchair	Ambulant	Dexterity	Visual	Auditory	Comprehension	note
✗ applicable		✗	✗	✗	✗	✗	✗	
1 ☐	Do the doors serve a <u>functional/ safety</u> purpose? (delete)	☐	☐	☐	☐	☐	☐	_____
2 ☐	Can they be readily distinguished?	☐	☐	☐	☐	☐	☐	_____
3 ☐	If glass, are they visible when shut?	☐	☐	☐	☐	☐	☐	_____
4 ☐	Can people <u>standing</u> or <u>sitting</u> in a wheelchair see each other and be seen from either side of the door? (delete)	☐	☐	☐	☐	☐	☐	_____
5 ☐	Does the clear opening width permit wheelchair access?	☐	☐	☐	☐	☐	☐	_____
6 ☐	On the opening side of the door is there sufficient space (300mm) to allow the door handle to be grasped and the door swing past a wheelchair footplate?	☐	☐	☐	☐	☐	☐	_____
7 ☐	Is any door furniture/ handle at a height for <u>standing/ sitting</u> use? (delete)	☐	☐	☐	☐	☐	☐	_____
8 ☐	Are door/ handles clearly distinguished?	☐	☐	☐	☐	☐	☐	_____
9 ☐	Can the door furniture/ handles be easily <u>operated/ grasped?</u> (delete)	☐	☐	☐	☐	☐	☐	_____
10 ☐	If <u>door closers/ mechanisms</u> (delete) are fitted do they provide the following:							
☐	(a) hold open (alarm linkage)?	☐	☐	☐	☐	☐	☐	_____
☐	(b) security linkage?	☐	☐	☐	☐	☐	☐	_____
☐	(c) delay-action closure?	☐	☐	☐	☐	☐	☐	_____
☐	(d) slow-action closure?	☐	☐	☐	☐	☐	☐	_____
☐	(e) minimum closure pressure?	☐	☐	☐	☐	☐	☐	_____
11 ☐	Is door/ mechanism function checked regularly?	☐	☐	☐	☐	☐	☐	_____

F

Accessibility Audit Report
Access Audit Checklist

Date _____

Location _____

✗ applicable

		Wheelchair	Ambulant	Dexterity	Visual	Auditory	Comprehension	note
		✗	✗	✗	✗	✗	✗	
1	☐ Is WC provision made for people with disabilities?	☐	☐	☐	☐	☐	☐	___
2	☐ Do all lavatory areas have slip-resistant floors?	☐	☐	☐	☐	☐	☐	___
3	☐ Are they easy to distinguish by colour contrast from the walls?	☐	☐	☐	☐	☐	☐	___
4	☐ Are all fittings readily distinguishable from the background?	☐	☐	☐	☐	☐	☐	___
5	☐ Are all door fittings/ locks easily gripped and operated?	☐	☐	☐	☐	☐	☐	___
6	☐ Can ambulant disabled people manoeuvre, raise and lower themselves in standard cubicles?	☐	☐	☐	☐	☐	☐	___
7	☐ Is provision made for wheelchair users?	☐	☐	☐	☐	☐	☐	___
8	☐ Is wheelchair approach free of <u>steps/ narrow doors/ obstructions</u>, etc? (delete)	☐	☐	☐	☐	☐	☐	___
9	☐ Is the location clearly signed?	☐	☐	☐	☐	☐	☐	___
10	☐ Is there sufficient space at entry to the compartment for wheelchair manoeuvre and door opening?	☐	☐	☐	☐	☐	☐	___
11	☐ Are the door fittings/ locks and light switches easily reached and operated?	☐	☐	☐	☐	☐	☐	___
12	☐ Is there an emergency call system and is someone designated to respond to it?	☐	☐	☐	☐	☐	☐	___
13	☐ Can the emergency call system be operated from floor level?	☐	☐	☐	☐	☐	☐	___
14	☐ Is the wheelchair WC compartment large enough to permit manoeuvre for <u>frontal/ lateral/ angled/ backward</u> transfer, <u>with</u> or <u>without</u> assistance? (delete)	☐	☐	☐	☐	☐	☐	___

© John Penton

continued

Accessibility Audit Report
Access Audit Checklist

Date _____

Location _____

✗ applicable

		Wheelchair	Ambulant	Dexterity	Visual	Auditory	Comprehension	note
		✗	✗	✗	✗	✗	✗	
15 ☐	Are the fittings arranged to facilitate these manoeuvres?	☐	☐	☐	☐	☐	☐	_____
16 ☐	Are handwashing and drying facilities within reach of someone seated on the WC?	☐	☐	☐	☐	☐	☐	_____
17 ☐	Is the tap appropriate for use by someone with limited dexterity, grip or strength?	☐	☐	☐	☐	☐	☐	_____
18 ☐	Are suitable grab rails fitted in all the appropriate positions to facilitate use of the WC?	☐	☐	☐	☐	☐	☐	_____
19 ☐	Is the manoeuvring area free of obstruction, eg boxed-in pipework/ radiators/ cleaners' equipment/ disposal bins/ occasional storage, etc, and is a difficulty caused by the activity of service contractors? (delete)	☐	☐	☐	☐	☐	☐	_____
20 ☐	If there is more than one standard layout WC compartment provided are they handed to offer a left-sided approach and a right-sided approach?	☐	☐	☐	☐	☐	☐	_____

G

Accessibility Audit Report
Access Audit Checklist

Date _____

Location _____

	Wheelchair	Ambulant	Dexterity	Visual	Auditory	Comprehension	note
✗ applicable	✗	✗	✗	✗	✗	✗	
1 Is any <u>refreshment facility/ meetings space/ seminar room/ counselling room</u> accessible to all users, including those with hearing impairments? (delete)	☐	☐	☐	☐	☐	☐	____
2 If there is fixed <u>seating/ tables</u> is there space for wheelchair users where they can sit with their carers or colleagues? (delete)	☐	☐	☐	☐	☐	☐	____
3 Can wheelchair users and other disabled people approach and use <u>food service areas/ vending machines/ cash points/ information points/ chapel</u> unimpeded? (delete)	☐	☐	☐	☐	☐	☐	____
4 Is it possible for people with disabilities to serve as volunteers?	☐	☐	☐	☐	☐	☐	____
5 Are all fittings readily distinguishable from their background?	☐	☐	☐	☐	☐	☐	____
6 Where there are <u>retail outlets</u> are they <u>visible/ signed/ reachable/ accessible</u> for people with disabilities? (delete)	☐	☐	☐	☐	☐	☐	____
7 In any <u>waiting area/ place of assembly</u> do tables and chairs and their layout allow for use by wheelchair users and people with sensory disabilities? (delete)	☐	☐	☐	☐	☐	☐	____
8 In any staff/ volunteer kitchen is it suitable for use by people with disabilities, including wheelchair users, with <u>slip-resistant floor/ reduced level kithcen units</u> and <u>sink</u> and <u>lever/ toggle action taps</u>? (delete)	☐	☐	☐	☐	☐	☐	____
9 Are all relevant locations clearly signed? **See checklist J**	☐	☐	☐	☐	☐	☐	____

H

Accessibility Audit Report
Access Audit Checklist

Date _____

Location _____

✗ applicable

	Wheelchair ✗	Ambulant ✗	Dexterity ✗	Visual ✗	Auditory ✗	Comprehension ✗	note
1 Is the building equipped to provide hearing assistance with induction loop/ infrared systems? (delete)	☐	☐	☐	☐	☐	☐	____
2 Does the lighting installation of the building take in to account the needs of people with visual disabilities?	☐	☐	☐	☐	☐	☐	____
3 Is there a tactile plan of the building?	☐	☐	☐	☐	☐	☐	____
4 Are there large-print versions of information about the building and its activities available?	☐	☐	☐	☐	☐	☐	____
5 Is there Braille information available for people with visual disabilities?	☐	☐	☐	☐	☐	☐	____
6 Is there an audio version of information about the building available?	☐	☐	☐	☐	☐	☐	____
7 Where there are staff and volunteers available in the building at reception/ information points/ refreshment facilities/ chapel/ counselling services/ retail outlets are they trained in communication with people with physical and sensory disabilities? (delete)	☐	☐	☐	☐	☐	☐	____
8 Where payphones are provided do they have hearing aid couplers?	☐	☐	☐	☐	☐	☐	____
9 Are all relevant location clearly signed?	☐	☐	☐	☐	☐	☐	____
10 Does the signage system incorporate colour/ tone/ contrast and upper and lower case lettering? (delete)	☐	☐	☐	☐	☐	☐	____

J

© John Penton

Accessibility Audit Report
Access Audit Checklist

Date _____

Location _____

✗ applicable

		Wheelchair	Ambulant	Dexterity	Visual	Auditory	Comprehension	note
		✗	✗	✗	✗	✗	✗	
1	☐ Is there a <u>visible</u> as well as <u>audible</u> fire alarm system? (delete)	☐	☐	☐	☐	☐	☐	_____
2	☐ Are final exit routes as accessible to all, including wheelchair users, as are the entry routes?	☐	☐	☐	☐	☐	☐	_____
3	☐ Is evacuation from <u>upper</u> and <u>lower</u> levels possible using an <u>evacuation lift/ platform lift</u> with a protected power supply? (delete)	☐	☐	☐	☐	☐	☐	_____
4	☐ If people with disabilities can not evacuate from the building independently are designated and signed refuges available for them?	☐	☐	☐	☐	☐	☐	_____
5	☐ If refuges are available are they equipped with 'carry-chairs'?	☐	☐	☐	☐	☐	☐	_____
6	☐ Is there a 'management evacuation strategy' for staff, volunteers and visitors, and are staff trained in procedures for evacuation of people with disabilities, including the checking and clearance of refuges?	☐	☐	☐	☐	☐	☐	_____
7	☐ Is any 'evacuation plan' checked regularly for its effectiveness?	☐	☐	☐	☐	☐	☐	_____
8	☐ Are evacuation routes checked routinely and regularly for freedom from <u>combustible materials/ obstacles/ locked doors</u>? (delete)	☐	☐	☐	☐	☐	☐	_____
9	☐ Are all fire warning devices and detectors checked routinely and regularly?	☐	☐	☐	☐	☐	☐	_____

© John Penton

125

Accessibility Audit Report
Access Audit Checklist

Date

Location

	Wheelchair	Ambulant	Dexterity	Visual	Auditory	Comprehension	note
✗ applicable	✗	✗	✗	✗	✗	✗	
1 ☐	☐	☐	☐	☐	☐	☐	
2 ☐	☐	☐	☐	☐	☐	☐	
3 ☐	☐	☐	☐	☐	☐	☐	
4 ☐	☐	☐	☐	☐	☐	☐	
5 ☐	☐	☐	☐	☐	☐	☐	
6 ☐	☐	☐	☐	☐	☐	☐	
7 ☐	☐	☐	☐	☐	☐	☐	
8 ☐	☐	☐	☐	☐	☐	☐	
9 ☐	☐	☐	☐	☐	☐	☐	
10 ☐	☐	☐	☐	☐	☐	☐	

S

© John Penton

continued

Accessibility Audit Report
Access Audit Checklist

Date _____

Location _____

✗ applicable

	Wheelchair	Ambulant	Dexterity	Visual	Auditory	Comprehension	note
	✗	✗	✗	✗	✗	✗	
11 ☐	☐	☐	☐	☐	☐	☐	
12 ☐	☐	☐	☐	☐	☐	☐	
13 ☐	☐	☐	☐	☐	☐	☐	
14 ☐	☐	☐	☐	☐	☐	☐	
15 ☐	☐	☐	☐	☐	☐	☐	
16 ☐	☐	☐	☐	☐	☐	☐	
17 ☐	☐	☐	☐	☐	☐	☐	
18 ☐	☐	☐	☐	☐	☐	☐	
19 ☐	☐	☐	☐	☐	☐	☐	
20 ☐	☐	☐	☐	☐	☐	☐	

S

Accessibility Audit Report
Access Audit Checklist

Date _____

Location _____

Cross Reference: _____ / Sheet _____ / Page No _____

Details

AN